PAS
FIRS
TIME

A Macdonald Orbis BOOK

First published in Great Britain in 1985
by Orbis Publishing Limited, London

Reprinted 1985 by Orbis Publishing Limited

Reprinted 1986, 1989 by Macdonald & Co (Publishers) Ltd
London & Sydney
a member of Maxwell Pergamon Publishing Corporation plc

ISBN 0-356-142736

This book was devised and produced by
Templar Publishing Limited,
Dorking, Surrey.

Editor: Lucy Baker
Designer: Mick McCarthy
Typeset by Templar Type
Printed in Spain by Cayfosa, Barcelona

Macdonald & Co (Publishers) Ltd
66-73 Shoe Lane
London EC4P 4AB

DEREK FAIRMAN

PASS FIRST TIME

CONSULTANT EDITOR
PETER RUSSELL
GENERAL SECRETARY OF THE DRIVING INSTRUCTORS' ASSOCIATION

CARTOONS BY COLLEEN PAYNE

Macdonald Orbis

INTRODUCTION

Each year between 1.8 million and 1.9 million people in Britain take a driving test. The overall fail rate is 52%, but among those taking it for the first time the fail rate is much higher – about 65% in fact. One of the most important reasons for this is that these people have not been prepared for exactly what happens in the test itself.

Knowing precisely what is expected of you is the first step to being confident when you get into the car with your examiner. It can also help you to concentrate beforehand on the manoeuvres most crucial to your success.

But what exactly is expected in the test? That's what this book is all about. It explains precisely what the examiner is looking for during all the important manoeuvres, and which major points are likely to contribute to a pass.

Of course, there's a lot more in the book that will help you to prepare yourself, as well as handy tips, useful information and reassurance on a whole host of questions.

The first two sections of the book deal with general points useful for pre-test preparations, anticipating questions that might be worrying you.

The third section deals specifically with the Driving Test and includes easy-to-follow Action Sequences that act as memory-joggers to the correct procedures to follow.

The fourth section looks at some of the more unusual pitfalls that can spoil your chances unless you are prepared for them.

Finally, in section five, we look at the laws you must abide by if you want to hold on to your licence.

What will become clear as you read this book is that "care and control" is the keynote to test success. Care means being alert to other road users, being observant and always being ready to take precautions. Control means exactly what it says – you must control the car, not let the car control you.

Finally, Good luck!

CONTENTS

FOREWORD

For fifty years now, people have needed to pass a test of 'competence' before they have been allowed to drive without supervision. It is the simplest and most basic test of driving skill in the country, and yet it has been shrouded in mystery just because so many people manage to fail.

Almost every driver has his own horror story about the driving test. Learner drivers are often regaled with tales of examiners who 'love to fail you'. And yet nothing could be further from the truth. The only rule that a driving examiner must apply to the test is:
"If the error which has just been made were to be the only error made during the test, is it sufficiently serious to mean that the candidate has proved he is not yet competent and safe enough to drive on his own?"

If the answer is yes, then very reluctantly the examiner has to write on the back of his marking sheet exactly why he believes it, and must also mark the candidate's sheet to the same effect.

Each different error which is sufficiently serious is marked, and these are the only ones marked on that form. But it is worth repeating that the candidate fails him (or her) self; the examiner would far prefer them to pass.

The purpose of this book is to explain exactly what happens on the driving test. And to take some of the awe out of the test, it makes effective use of cartoons. Read the book through, smile at the cartoons, but take note of the underlying message which is given to you and know exactly what to expect on your test.

An Approved Driving Instructor, especially one who has passed his Diploma in Driving Instruction, will have been able to act the role of the examiner for you; and I know from my own experience of over 3,500 driving test passes, that all my pupils used to say to me:
"The test was easy because the examiner was so much nicer to me than you were; and I simply followed the examiner's directions by driving in the manner in which you had taught me".

This book backs up everything you should have been taught – so when your test arrives you know what to expect and you are confident that you can do everything that is required without any help or guidance.

This book can remove any worries you have. And if you are competent and prepared for everything that can happen, you'll PASS FIRST TIME.

Peter Russell
General Secretary – DRIVING INSTRUCTORS' ASSOCIATION

1
STARTER'S ORDERS

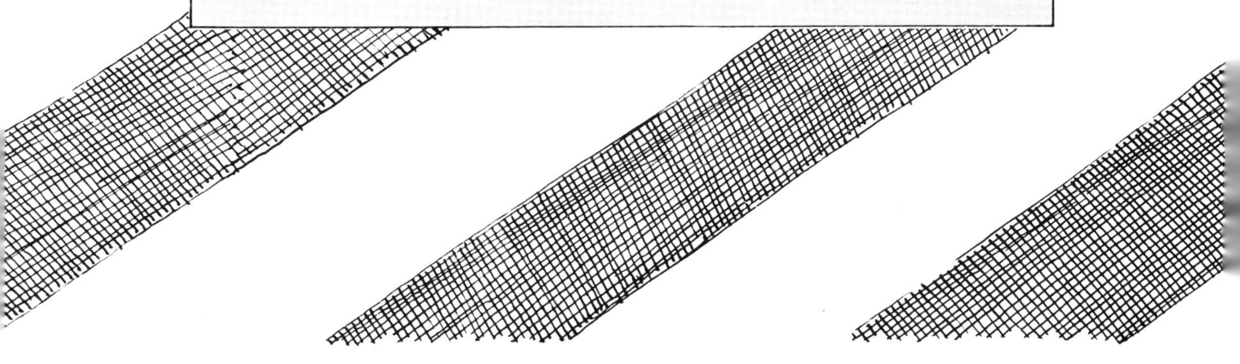

APPLYING FOR YOUR TEST

To apply for your driving test you must get a form from your local post office. Fill it in and select two of the listed test centres – you are given a first and second choice. Post the form off, enclosing the fee, and within a matter of weeks you should receive a card telling you the time and place of your test.

It's worth finding out the usual waiting time for a test. In some areas you'll be given a date shortly following that of your application. But in others, you may have months to wait. If this is the case, consider applying for your test date as soon as you start to learn to drive. With luck, the date will coincide with the point at which you're capable and confident of taking the test. If not, all you have to do is fill in the card cancelling the appointment (at least a week before the date). You will then be given another date, hopefully involving only a short waiting time.

Once the date is booked, make sure your instructor knows so he can plan your lessons accordingly. If you aren't using an instructor for regular lessons, it's usually worth booking one or two sessions in the final couple of weeks' run-up to the test. This should help to pinpoint any shortcomings in your driving technique and give you enough time to improve.

KNOW YOUR ROUTE

It's useful to know your test area as well as possible in advance. Many towns have unique road systems. The locals know what's going on, but the outsider is baffled. So acquaint yourself, make sure you understand its one-way systems, double roundabouts etc. If possible drive around at the same time of day as your test. One-way streets, sharp corners, school crossings or roads with heavy traffic are all worth knowing in advance. At the same time, check if the test centre has parking facilities, and if not, where the nearest parking spots are located.

WATCHING THE WEATHER

Many learner drivers prefer not to practise when the weather's bad. It is quite understandable, but remember that driving tests are usually only cancelled if conditions are actually dangerous.

Driving tests may be cancelled because of weather conditions which do not allow the test to be conducted on a fair and equable basis. For instance, even a light fall of snow can mean tests are cancelled because it becomes impossible to see the white lines on the road. Theretore the examiner cannot tell how you would behave if the road surface was clear. Thick fog is another reason. And, of course, tests cannot be conducted on really icy roads. Rain is not normally regarded as an impediment, so it is important that you can cope with wet, slippery roads. And that means you need to have some experience of driving in the wet. Even in the summer, you can't count on good weather blessing your test day!

If you're unable to reach the test centre because of bad weather, telephone them to let them know. Similarly, if you are doubtful about whether the tests are running, ring and check before you leave home. Any test cancelled for such reasons will be given priority in rebooking, and you'll get a revised date as soon as possible free of charge. There's usually someone at the centre about 10 minutes before tests begin or between 8.45am and 9.45am each morning.

Test times are generally:

AM	9.00	9.45	10.45	11.30	12.15
PM	2.00	2.45	3.30	(4.15 in Summer)	

(But note that these times will alter early in 1987 to enable Examiners to conduct 8 tests per day instead of 9).

In certain areas in the country tests are conducted at slightly different times. But your driving test appointment card gives you all the details of the place, date and time so, if you are in any doubt, follow what your card says.

FIRST IMPRESSIONS

A clean car is one of the best ways of giving your examiner a good first impression. But it goes further than that because a neglected car is unlikely to be in tip-top working order. If you have a choice of cars for your test, and you are happy driving all of them, pick the most respectable and road worthy. If you have only your own car for the purpose, then make sure it's clean and well maintained.

Here's a quick guide of things to check before you take your test. Remember, an unroadworthy car is an instant fail and running out of petrol an immediate cancellation so make sure that:

- Windows and mirrors are clean to ensure clear vision. Side mirrors must be properly adjusted and undamaged.
- Horn, speedo, windscreen washers and wipers are in working order.
- Headlights, sidelights and indicators are clean and in working order.
- Seat belts are clean and securely fitted.
- You have plenty of oil, water, and petrol in the car.
- You carry a spare fuse (just in case!) and know where it goes.
- Battery is topped up and the connections are clean and secure.
- Tyres are inflated to the correct pressure and have legal tread.
- Brakes and steering are properly adjusted.
- 'L' plates are clearly displayed at the front and back of your car.

WHAT TO WEAR

You might think that what you wear has little to do with the way you drive. But it can. For example, thin soled shoes allow more sensitivity with the pedals, while thick soles can make you clumsy. Very low or flat shoes are a great improvement on heels, which can get caught up in things like floor mats and make driving difficult. Although very short people or people with short legs may find it advantageous to wear heeled shoes. Trousers have a great advantage over dresses too (femininity out the window!). Full skirts can get in the way of the gear lever and hand brake; tight or clinging skirts can leave you thinking more of how much leg you are showing than of your driving. Low necklines are unlikely to give you any advantage either!

Another niggling point is sleeves. Very wide sleeves can cause havoc with gear or indicator levers. Last point, your hair. If you can see out of both eyes, and it doesn't threaten to fall across your face, that's fine. But if there is a problem, put it up or hold it back with a band.

CAN YOUR INSTRUCTOR COME TOO?

Yes, you can have your instructor with you. So if the thought of being alone with the examiner terrifies you, stop worrying. However, he won't be able to advise you at all during the test.

Ask the examiner if it is possible for your instructor to sit in on the test. If he agrees, then your instructor may sit in the back of the car, but the examiner will specifically tell him that he must take no part in the test, except as an observer. If you ask your instructor first, you will probably find that he would rather not sit in, unless he wants to for his own benefit.

What you should ask yourself, is *why* do you want your instructor to sit in? If it's because you don't feel competent yet, a few extra lessons with your instructor acting the role of a totally uninvolved supervisor may solve your problems.

THE SUPERVISING EXAMINER

The one occasion when it would not be possible for your instructor to sit in with you during the test is when the examiner is having his own standards checked by the Department of Transport. About every six weeks or so, each driving examiner is required to have his own work supervised to ensure that all tests are conducted in the same way. So don't be surprised to find that you have two examiners on test with you. However, the test will be no more difficult. As an added bonus, you can take comfort from knowing that you are not the only person being tested.

If you really do not want to have a second examiner in the car, you are invited to say so; but now you know the reason why, you are less likely to object. There is no way that having a second examiner can affect the result at all.

TAKING ADVANTAGE OF THE EXAMINER

Once strapped in, the examiner may appear to be open to seduction. If you are tempted to win his favour in a somewhat 'irregular' fashion, forget it! You will only embarrass or annoy him. Neither will work in your favour.

BRIBERY!

Don't even contemplate bribery. The chances are that the suggestion will not be taken lightly, and you could wind up in serious trouble. The test exists to certify you've reached the necessary standard to be safe on the roads. If you don't make this stage honestly then it's dangerous (and unfair to others) for you to hold a licence.

MAKING IT A SMOOTH RIDE

During your whole test, try and give the examiner a smooth ride. Don't accelerate madly or stop suddenly. The examiner has at least eight tests each working day and a smooth pleasant drive could tip the balance in your favour.

About once every other day, one of the examiner's driving tests has to end – in a hurry. Something that the candidate does worries the examiner so much that he is forced to take action. He would only do this in an effort to avoid an accident, but nevertheless it does happen.

Before taking *your* test, ensure that you have taken enough 'mock' driving tests with your instructor to *know* that you will be able to get round the route safely. If you are not sure, postpone the test.

SMOKING AND DRINKING ON TEST

If you are a smoker, then smoke in the waiting room *before* the test, even smoke in the car *after* the test, but under no circumstances should you even think of smoking *during* the test. It's not only rude, but potentially dangerous.

Unlike smoking, drinking and driving is not on at any time (see page 78). Not even a quick drink to fortify your nerves before the test please. Be warned: if the examiner gets the slightest whiff of drink on your breath the test will be abandoned.

UNUSUAL VEHICLES

Automatics are no different from manual cars as far as the test is concerned. (But they are often an advantage to learner drivers who find clutch control difficult.) However, once passed in an automatic, your licence is limited and you'll have to go through the whole test again before you are permitted to drive a manual car on your own.

It is possible to take your test in a left-hand drive car. The only difference during the test is that the examiner will expect you to pay extra attention to rear observation.

TEST ABANDONED

The examiner can terminate your test at any time for a number of reasons, without telling you why. Most commonly, however, it is one of three things...

- He considers you totally unsafe to drive without supervision.
- He considers the car unsafe.
- The car (or part of the car) has stopped working.

This step isn't taken lightly (if nothing else, it means the examiner will have to walk back to the centre!). You will be asked to stay with the car while the examiner goes back to inform your instructor. Everything will be extremely discreet and only you and your instructor will know what's happening.

GIVE WAY
Birmingham M10
Watford
London
30
DRIVER ON TEST L
349W91
ROAD WORKS AHEAD

2
ON THE ROAD

USING YOUR MIRROR

One of the most widespread causes of failure is not using the rear-view mirror properly. You need to be familiar with the road behind, and your mirror offers the only clear viewpoint. Some people call the mirror the 'third eye', and this is a very good description of it. You really must use your mirrors (all of them – including any door or side mirrors) *well before* you change your speed or your direction, at any time. Remember the most basic of all driving rules:
MIRROR... SIGNAL... MANOEUVRE
and make sure you apply it every time you are required to make any change in your driving. On your driving test, this means not just looking into the mirror, but acting on what you have seen.

Some people will tell you to move the mirror out of alignment so that you are forced to move your head each time you look. This is dangerous and foolish. Not only will you miss some occasions when you need to look, you may well end up as one of the 'examiner takes action' statistics.

MAKING PROGRESS

There's some jargon that comes up in a driving test. One example is the expression 'make progress'. This is just another way of saying drive at an appropriate speed, but *without hesitancy.*

Learners often tend to drive more slowly on test than during lessons with their instructor. If you do, remember that the examiner will mark you on how you drive now, *not* on how you have been driving before. If it was correct to do so with your instructor, you must also drive that way on your test. And after your test too, of course.

The only way to get this 'making progress' way of driving natural is to practise with someone who knows what they're doing, or rather what you should be doing. It's a matter of being confident and positive in both your driving ability and judgements.

ROAD POSITIONING AND DISTANCE

The usual safe position for your car to be in relation to the kerb is about a metre (or three feet if you are still an imperial thinker). A better way to remember this, is to think of a 'car door width'. Never drive closer than an open car door width to anything. You will know why the first time you see someone open a car door as you drive past. When passing or overtaking other vehicles make sure you have this clearance at all times. The only exception being for pedal cycles, especially if they are being ridden by children. Give them *even more* room. Imagine where they would be if they fell off, and allow them *that* amount of room if you can.

More important than the distance you keep from the kerb, however, is the distance you leave between your car and the one in front. At normal road speed (30 mph) it is recommended that a stopping gap of approximately five cars (75 feet) is left. Naturally, if your speed is faster, so the gap should be larger. When the roads are wet or icy, too, a much larger safety gap is needed.

If someone overtakes you, remember that he is now occupying 'your braking distance', and you may well have to slow down to give yourself the same safety margin you had before. If everyone wants to overtake you, especially if you are doing 30 mph in a 30 limit, bear in mind that it is better to have the lunatics in front of you, where you can see what they might be doing, rather than behind you inspecting your exhaust pipe!

Remember to hold the steering wheel at the ten-to-two (or quarter-to-three) position and pass it from one hand to the other. Never cross your hands and try not to go over the twelve o'clock mark either (this will count against you). Take both hands off the wheel and you've failed.

USE OF SPEED

Most drivers slip over the speed limit from time to time, but your driving test must NOT be one of those times. The examiner will fail you if he notices: it's classed as potentially dangerous. Try to maintain a steady speed just below the limit. And be cautious – road conditions may dictate an even lower speed.

CAR AND PAVEMENT DON'T GO!

Imagine driving along a narrow, winding road. An oncoming car appears. You know you can't pass safely, so what do you do? Drive on to the pavement until the car has passed? No.

The best solution is for you, or the other driver, to reverse back to a part of the road wide enough for two. Having said this, if another vehicle closes in behind you and the oncoming car seems unlikely to reverse, the examiner can instruct you to mount the pavement as the last solution.

HORN AND HEADLIGHTS

The horn is an audible warning of approach. You should use it to alert an unwary pedestrian or car that is about to pull out on you. But excessive or casual use can be taken as failure to read the road pattern, so it's best to avoid using it unless a real emergency crops up.

Similarly, headlights should be used in moderation. In daylight, headlights are only used to let another driver know you are there (which is actually the ONLY official required use).

During your test – and certainly during your lessons – someone is likely to flash their headlights at you to tell you something. If so, you must not act blindly on what you think they are telling you; but read into their signal what they obviously mean. If they are stopping to let you pass in front of them at a right turn, make sure that they have stopped, and that it is absolutely safe before you emerge in front or across them. Read their headlight signal as 'I am here', and then deduce from whatever else they are doing any extra meaning if you are able.

If you are being tested in the rain, remember that you are required to use dipped headlights if poor visibility demands it. Don't forget that it has to be your decision. The examiner is not there to remind you.

OBSERVATION

One of the worst things you can do is blindly follow the car in front. You can never presume that what's safe for him is also safe for you.

Look as far ahead as you can. This way you'll know what to expect and have time to decide if you need to slow down. This cautious, observant approach is necessary whatever the road situation and condition.

ANTICIPATION

Like constant observation, both behind and in front, anticipating the intentions of other drivers relieves a lot of the stress and strain of driving. Watch everyone carefully, particularly when approaching junctions and other hazard areas.

Above all, remember the bike. Bicycles and motorbikes can squeeze through gaps that cars would never think of attempting, and often they will. For this reason be extra careful if you are planning to change lanes. If necessary turn your head left and right to make sure you haven't missed one in your blind spots.

BEWARE OF CYCLISTS

Whether cyclists are a nuisance or not depends mainly upon where you live and the time of day. Either way, beware. If you don't give cyclists sufficient room as you pass them, you could easily fail yourself. Often they wobble precariously, so take this into account.

If a cyclist starts to move out into the road as you are approaching a junction, slow down to anticipate their next move.

ADEQUATE CLEARANCE

You'll find one of the most common obstacles in town driving is parked cars. As you approach these, look out for tell-tale signs of danger.

If someone's in the driving seat – are they about to open the door? If there's smoke coming from the exhaust – is the car about to pull out? If there are shadows between parked cars – is it a child about to cross the road?

Give all parked cars lots of clearance, and keep your eyes open.

STALLING

Stalling the engine (meaning when the engine stops and the car lurches to an ignominious stop) will not necessarily fail you. But the examiner will be marking you on the cause of the stall. If the cause was not a serious one you will still pass.

If you keep on stalling there could be two reasons. The first is that there is something wrong with the car – it may be in the wrong gear, or the handbrake may still be applied. The second is likely to be the way you are driving, with poor control of the clutch. If you are too tense, then you'll not be driving at your best. So as well as stalling, you're probably not even seeing what is around you. The answer has to be more practice, especially with 'mock' tests.

HOLES IN THE ROAD

Good observation doesn't just involve watching cars, bikes and people: there are also the roads themselves. The surface of a road can vary from dry to wet, from smooth to bumpy, all in a matter of seconds. Leaves, mud, bricks or holes all present potential problems. When approaching obstacles and holes, slow down and try to put the obstacle between your wheels (provided it's not too high). And remember, if this means altering your road position, look behind first. If you come up against slippery surfaces like ice patches or wet leaves, slow down.

ANIMALS IN THE ROAD

Apart from dogs straying onto the road, the most likely animal you'll meet is the horse. Horses are usually nervous. So give them a wide berth as you pass, slowing down and keeping engine revs to a minimum.

On country lanes, you may meet flocks of sheep or herds of cattle being driven to pasture. If you get caught behind them, don't get impatient, just trail behind very slowly and don't try to overtake. If they're approaching you, stop and allow them to pass. The examiner would expect you to pass in a sensible and controlled manner, and under no circumstances to sound your horn.

WHO HAS PRIORITY?

After the basic rule of 'KEEP LEFT', the next most important one to remember while driving is 'GIVE WAY'. Don't assume that anyone has a 'right' of way. The most you can hope for is that other road users will allow you to have priority, but don't take it for granted and never call it 'right of way'.

MEETING OTHER ROAD USERS

If you are driving along, and the road width narrows, for any reason whatever, you also have to take account of who has priority. If the obstruction is on your side, you must allow the oncoming traffic to clear before you can pass the obstruction. If the obstruction is on the other side, oncoming traffic may or may not decide to allow you priority. Your mother may have given you advice on this subject when you were a little child. "Don't push in front of people, it is rude". Wise mums will add, "You might get hurt".

Look out for road signs that may help you, especially the one that means: GIVE PRIORITY TO VEHICLES FROM THE OPPOSITE DIRECTION; and the other which means: PRIORITY OVER VEHICLES FROM THE OPPOSITE DIRECTION. Notice that the latter does *not* mean TAKE.

EMERGENCY VEHICLES

Emergency vehicles (fire engines, ambulances and police cars/bikes) can terrify any driver. If you hear a siren behind you, pull over in the correct manner. Once it's passed, check there are no vehicles in convoy (there often are).

ROAD MARKINGS

Road signs and markings are there to help you. They must always be obeyed. Once you understand them, you'll realise just how helpful they are, and like every other part of driving, they'll become second nature. But there is no easy way of learning their meaning. Study the Highway Code so that you are sure.

TRAFFIC SIGNS

Like road markings, traffic signs are there to help you. Once you understand all signs, markings and signals given by other road users or traffic controllers, you will benefit from them. The correct sequence of traffic lights is often questioned on the test, so make sure you know it.

ROAD SIGNALS

- Only use the signals shown in the Highway Code.
- Only give signals that help or warn other road users. And when indicating, make sure that you give the correct direction, in good time, and that your indicator corrects itself.
- Learn and obey all arm signals given by police officers, traffic wardens directing traffic, and school crossing patrols.
- Although no longer required as a specific item on the test, arm signals used by drivers should be learnt and practised. You could be asked to demonstrate your knowledge of them at the test centre.
- On approaching a zebra crossing where people are waiting, the slowing down arm signal should be used.

PEDESTRIANS AND CROSSINGS

Pedestrians are probably the biggest single worry in town driving, the elderly and young in particular. Give them plenty of room and always be prepared to stop. When turning into a road, always give way to crossing pedestrians.

Pedestrian crossings require just as much attention. As you approach a zebra crossing, slow down in plenty of time to see if people are waiting. If not, proceed normally. Show waiting pedestrians you are slowing down by giving an arm signal if you get the opportunity. But make sure that they do really want to cross and that they see you do it. If a pedestrian's foot is on the crossing, then they automatically have priority. Sadly, you often find that you are the only one likely to give it to them. Avoid stopping suddenly; this might cause the car behind to hit or overtake you. Plan your approach with more care. Never invite or beckon pedestrians to cross. In traffic queues, leave all crossings clear.

Slow down for pelican lights and never cross until all is clear. Provided it is safe, you can continue whilst the amber light is flashing, but do look out for last minute pedestrians who may rush out.

TEST CENTRE
BEST OF LUCK!
GOOD LUCK!
HOPE YOU PASS!
CGP001

3

TAKING THE TEST

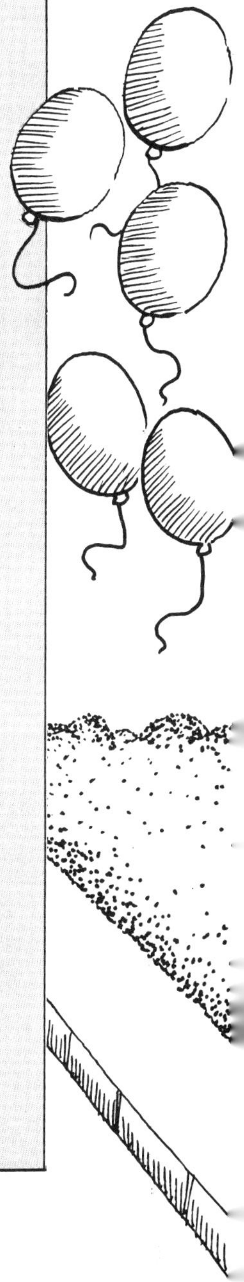

The test centre

The waiting room

"Good morning, Mr Candidate"

"Move off when you are ready, please"

"At the end of the road turn left please"

"Take the first road on the left please"

"Take the second road on the left please"

"At the end of the road turn right please"

"Follow the road ahead..." (Crossroads)

"Take the second exit at the roundabout"

"...shortly I shall ask you to stop as in an emergency..."

"Pull up on the left, at a convenient place"

"Move off when you are ready..."

"Move off when you are ready..." (Hill start – up)

"Move off when you are ready..." (Hill start – down)

"...I should like you to reverse..." (to the left)

"...I should like you to reverse..." (to the right)

"I'd like you to turn your car..."

"...I should now like to ask you some questions..."

"...I'm pleased to tell you that you have passed..."

"...I'm sorry you haven't passed..."

Both the preceding sections were designed to familiarise you with the rules and codes of conduct on the road. Now let's look at the big event itself – the test. Each of the important manoeuvres that feature in the test are explained briefly. This is then followed by a summary of what the examiner wants to see. And finally, there's an 'Action Sequence' telling you, step-by-step, how the exercise should be completed. (There's a diagram showing the route your car should take, too.) All this will give you a clear idea of what's involved in the test. You'll realise how level-headedness should be all that's needed to pass. That is, if you're up to the right driving standard.

For the test itself you'll need:

Your provisional licence.

Your test card giving the time and place of your test.

A car which is both safe and legal. Legal, in this case, means the vehicle must have a current MOT certificate and tax disc, and be insured for you to drive. (Don't forget your 'L' plates either.) The car can be your own or provided by the driving school – the test centre does not supply cars.

And, of course, a reasonable driving proficiency!

THE TEST CENTRE

On the day of judgement, make sure you set off in good time. Ideally you want to arrive about ten minutes before starting time. If you're late, you not only run the risk of missing your appointment, but arriving at the last minute will also add to your nervousness – not the best psychological condition for taking your test.

When you get to the test centre, park in a convenient position, so you can easily pull away! If you're parking in the road, face towards the simplest junction.

Not all centres have their own toilet facilities, although the whereabouts of those nearby are always displayed on a notice board. It's best to go before you set out for your test. That way you can't be caught out.

THE WAITING ROOM

Rather like a dentist's waiting room, the test centre will be full of people anxiously waiting for their name to be called. Many might even prefer to be at the dentist!

Wait patiently. If you're a smoker, this is the time for that last puff. As the clock moves on to the appointed time the examiners will troop in...

"GOOD MORNING, MR CANDIDATE"

Look for the examiner who calls your name, and go over to him.

He will then confirm your name and ask you to sign his daily journal. This is the list of test candidates that he has on the day.

"WOULD YOU SIGN AGAINST YOUR NAME PLEASE."

As you sign he will compare the signature with that on your test application form, so if you are not the right person he can stop the test.

"WILL YOU LEAD THE WAY TO YOUR VEHICLE PLEASE."

As you start to walk out of the room he will follow. He avoids being too close to you, but he also needs to find out one more thing before the test can start.

"HAVE YOU ANY PHYSICAL DISABILITY THAT ISN'T DECLARED ON YOUR APPLICATION?"

This is not a trick, and he is not being funny. But some people may well have incurred a disability since they filled in the application form, and others may have a disability which they were too shy or forgetful to tell their instructor. If you do have any, tell him. It makes his job easier, and may in some way make the test easier for you too.

If not, say "NO".

Outside the test centre he will ask you to identify your car.

"WHICH IS YOUR VEHICLE, PLEASE?"

This is a prelim to the eyesight test. After all, he wouldn't want to test you on your own numberplate! He will ask you to read the numberplate of a vehicle which is more than 67 feet away.

"CAN YOU READ TO ME THE NUMBER OF THAT CAR PLEASE."

The examiner will point out a car and may add some clue to help you identify it, for example "...the red one over there".

It may be necessary for him to go over to the vehicle with you to read the number. If you were not able to read the numberplate correctly he must follow a set procedure of testing your eyesight, at a measured distance of 67 feet for the modern, smaller plates with numbers 3⅛ inches high or 75 feet for the older numberplates 3½ inches high.

If you are still unable to read a number, then you have wasted your driving test fee, plus anything you've spent on lessons. And you are breaking the law.

Presuming you have identified the number correctly, he'll ask you to get into your car.

"WILL YOU GET INTO YOUR VEHICLE PLEASE, AND WAIT FOR ME – I WON'T BE A MOMENT."

When you have got into the car, you may be surprised to find that the examiner is interested in what you are driving. He is. He needs to know the make, the model, and other relevant details. All of this must be written on the back of his form.

When he does get into the car with you, he'll also need to complete some brief details about you too. When he starts writing his brief description, don't try to read what he says about you. For one thing you might discover he doesn't know the difference between 'well proportioned' and 'plump'. Secondly he won't want you to be interested in what he is doing. He is testing you. And the practical part of the driving test is about to begin.

"MOVE OFF WHEN YOU ARE READY PLEASE"

"I SHALL ASK YOU TO FOLLOW THE ROAD AHEAD, OR AS DIRECTION SIGNS INDICATE, UNLESS I WANT YOU TO TURN. I'LL TELL YOU WHICH WAY IN GOOD TIME."

"MOVE OFF WHEN YOU ARE READY PLEASE."

This is where the fun and games begin. It's where you need to remember everything you have learned, and put it all into practice. Before starting your car do the correct safety checks explained opposite, then patiently turn the key and give a small amount of acceleration. Don't panic if the engine doesn't catch immediately.

Once your engine's going, the examiner will ask you to follow the road unless signs direct you otherwise, or until he asks you to turn, all of which will happen in good time. Bear in mind that this will mean going straight on at roundabouts or similar, and following one-way systems until further instructions are given. Listen out for any directions the examiner may give. Rest assured, they will all be clear and simple.

Remember too that he needs to fill in his form with all the items mentioned before, so don't worry if he appears to be doing a lot of writing at the beginning of the test. He has to follow the Department of Transport's guidelines absolutely.

What the examiner is looking for

1. The usual precautions to starting the engine, especially that your handbrake is on and the gear lever in neutral, but also that your door is correctly shut, you are seated comfortably, belted in and can see clearly out of all mirrors.

2. Good observation all round the car, and indication if necessary, before pulling away.

3. A safe exit and a smooth acceleration up to normal road speed.

ACTION SEQUENCE

Moving off

Once the examiner is settled in beside you, the real driving test begins. Make sure you follow the pre-start routine explained below before starting the engine.

The pre-start routine is to ensure that it is safe to start your car. Remember to check the same points if you stall the engine or are asked to stop and then start again during any part of your test.

When the examiner is sitting beside you, display the following safety checks before starting the engine:

1 Make sure your car door is firmly shut and that both the examiner and you have fastened your seat belts, as required by law.

2 Ensure that you can reach all pedals comfortably, and that you can see clearly out of the front of your car and through your rear view mirror.

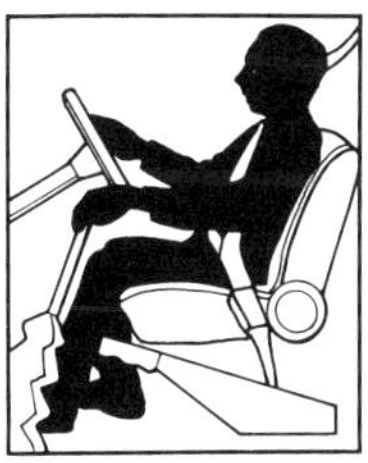

3 Make sure the gear stick is in neutral and the handbrake is firmly applied. This should be the case whenever your car is stationary.

Start your car. Turn the ignition and gently press the accelerator to allow your engine to start. If it's very cold you could pull the choke out, but remember to cancel it immediately after you have started. The engine will not be that cold if you drove it to the test centre a few minutes earlier.

Look all round. Depending on where and how you are parked, check all round for pedestrians and oncoming cars. If there is anything about, indicate your intention to pull away.

Pull away. When all is clear, engage first gear and release the handbrake. Take a final look over your shoulder before pulling smoothly away.

"AT THE END OF THE ROAD TURN LEFT PLEASE"

Turning out of a T-junction is likely to be one of the first manoeuvres you make (especially if the test centre has parking facilities). Naturally, a right-hand turn would require more attention than a left, but the steps to follow are similar.

Your examiner will give you a direction well in advance. Don't panic, your test is only just beginning...

What the examiner is looking for

1. Use of your mirror before signalling.

2. The correct indication.

3. A smooth stop – if necessary, at an appropriate position at the junction.

4. Thorough observation to the right, left and right again before proceeding.

5. Handbrake on and car put into neutral if you have to wait.

6. Smooth acceleration up to the appropriate speed.

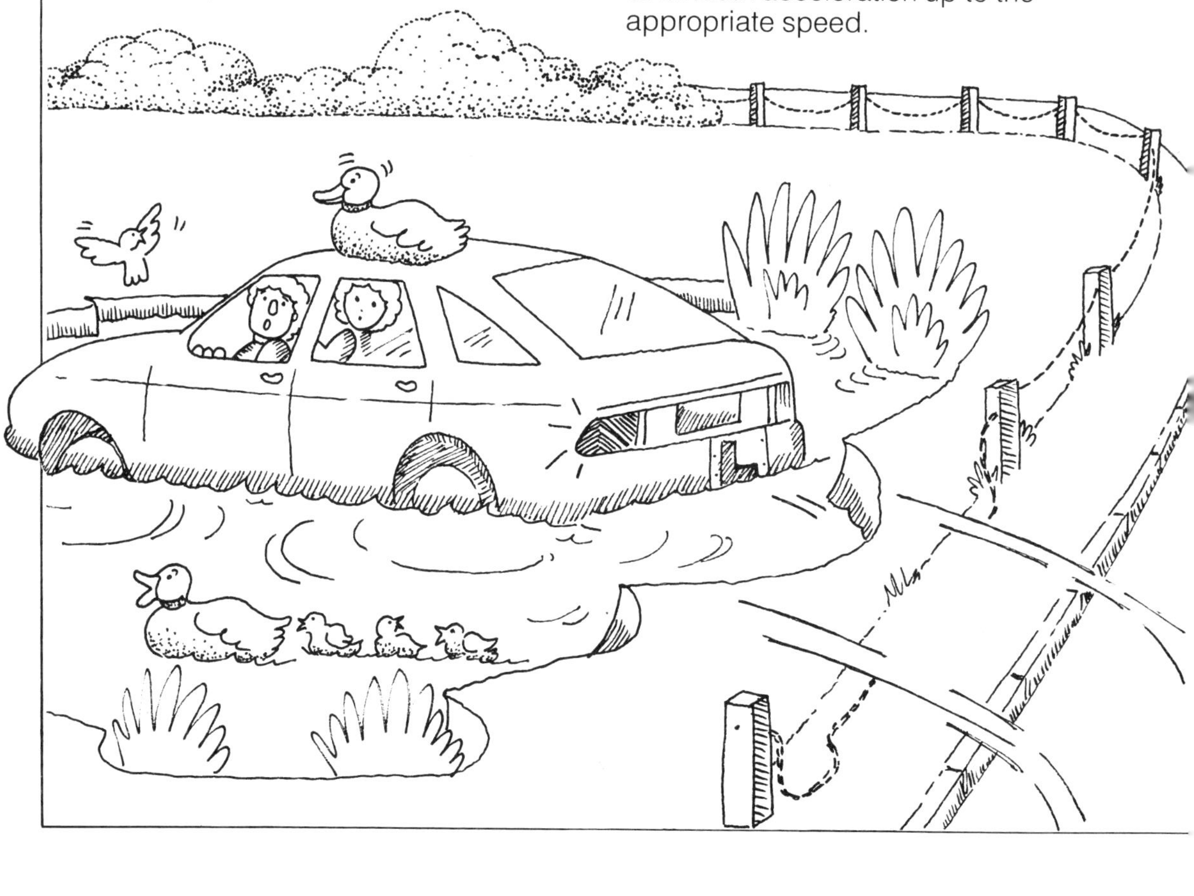

ACTION SEQUENCE

The procedure for a left or right-hand turn

The course to take for either a left or right-hand turn is shown here. Note, in particular, the position for the start of the manoeuvre.

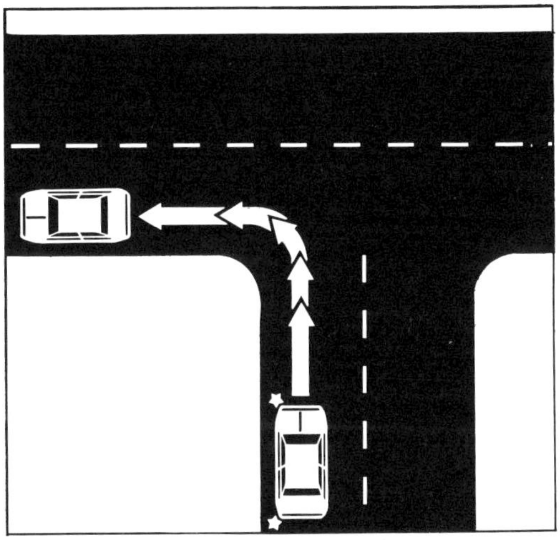

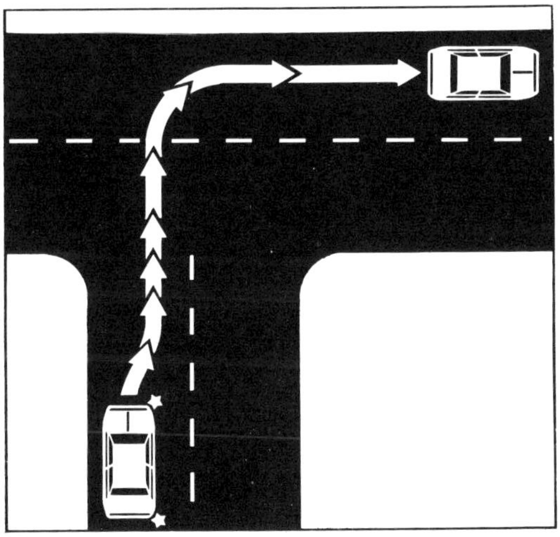

Look in your mirror to see what's happening behind. There could be a bike behind that may slip in beside you and you will need to know it's there to be safe.

Signal. Indicate which way you're going to turn. Drivers behind will then know where best to place themselves.

Position your car. When turning left, you need only keep to the left of the lane, which is where you should be already, before stopping. But if you are turning right, then a move to the right of the lane will be necessary.

Look in both directions. If the road isn't a busy one, then a look to your right, left and then right again should tell you if it's safe to pull out. However, if it isn't safe, then you must continue looking from one direction to the other until you're sure the path is clear.

Pull away. You may have to wait quite a while at a busy junction. If this is the case, put your handbrake on and take the car out of gear while you wait. Then as you see a clearing emerge, engage gear and be ready to release the handbrake.

"TAKE THE FIRST ROAD ON THE LEFT PLEASE"

When you're told to take the next road, be it right or left, the first thing to do is locate its whereabouts. There are usually road signs to help you, but if not there are obvious clues. Gaps between houses or shops, a strip of sunlight across the road, or another car signalling or appearing from nowhere are all tell-tale signs. Make sure you slow right down if the road you're entering has a blind corner.

What the examiner is looking for

1. Use of your mirror before signalling.

2. The correct indication in good time.

3. Regulation of speed using brakes and/ or appropriate gears.

4. A smooth turn with precise steering. (If you were turning right, good observation and consideration for approaching traffic would also be expected.)

5. A safe entry onto the new road and smooth acceleration up to normal road speed.

ACTION SEQUENCE

Turning off to the left or right

The positioning for both a left and right-hand turn are shown below. Make sure you don't cut corners or approach at an unsafe speed. If you are turning right, move to the right of the lane after indicating.

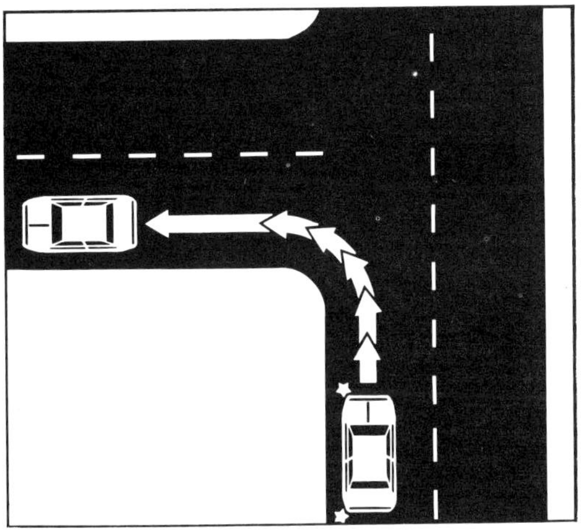

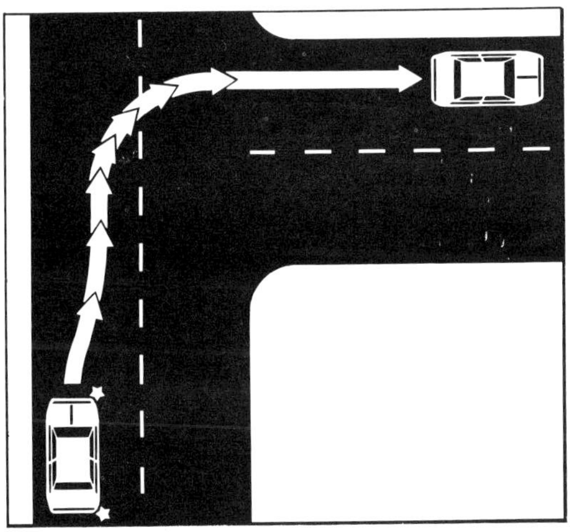

Look all round. You must know the location of your turning so as not to slow down ages before or drive straight past it. As with any other manoeuvre, check the situation behind before changing speed, position, or even indicating.

Signal, get into position and slow down. Indicate your intentions to all around. Then, using your gears as well as your brakes, slow down. Remember for a right hand turn you might have to stop completely. And even on the left turn you'll need to slow right down.

Check the road. Little observation is needed before you take the left turn but once around the corner you'll need to quickly assess whether it's safe to proceed. There's a different story for a right turn. You will have to judge carefully the speed of any oncoming traffic as you mustn't disrupt another car's path. And you will also have to make sure that you have easy access into the new road.

Steer round the corner. When turning, follow the line of the kerb. If you are turning right, you will have to position your car so that you enter the new road just left of the centre line. Don't try to cut corners.

"TAKE THE SECOND ROAD ON THE LEFT PLEASE"

When the examiner asks you to take the second turning, you'll need to look quite a way up the road so that you can rapidly identify which one he means. If there is any danger of confusion, he will identify it for you, often by adding "This is the first".

It's worth mentioning that some right and left hand turns are actually crossroads. Keep a sharp eye out if this is the case. Being on the main road you have priority, but always try to anticipate any moves by other drivers which might cross your path.

What the examiner is looking for

1. Use of your mirror before signalling.

2. Precise and clear indicating, bearing in mind the position of the first road, to avoid confusing nearby traffic.

3. Regulation of speed using brakes and/or appropriate gears.

4. A smooth turn with precise steering. And, if you were turning right, good observation and consideration of approaching traffic.

5. A safe entry onto the new road and smooth acceleration up to normal road speed.

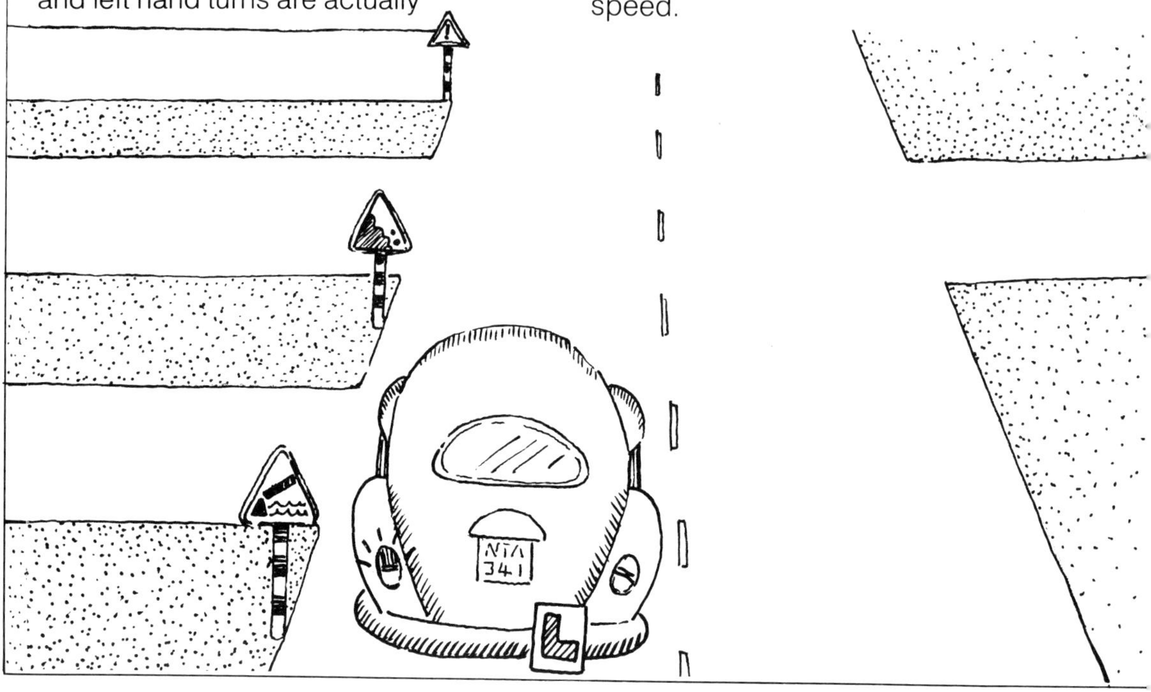

ACTION SEQUENCE

Taking a second left or right

Below you can see the correct route to take for a second left or right-hand turn. Timing the indicating correctly is vital when the two roads lie close together. It should begin just as you pass the entrance to the first turning, as shown.

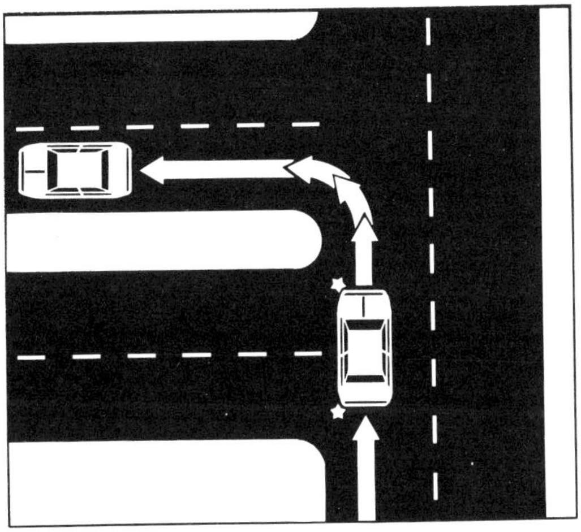

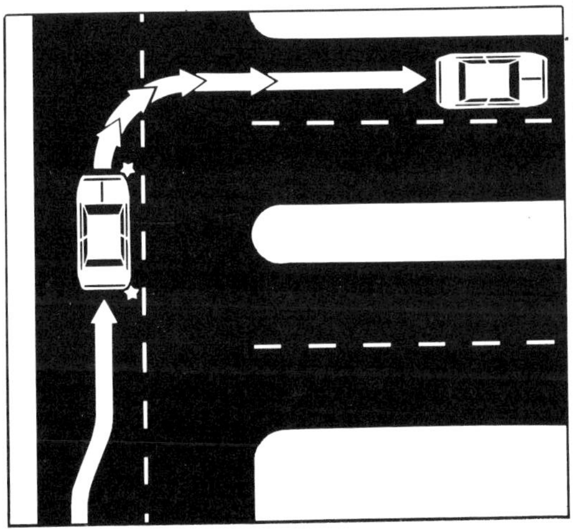

Look all round. Find the location of your turning before anything else. You'll be able to time things correctly once you know its whereabouts. And then check your mirror as a precaution.

Signal, get into position and slow down. Indicating must be perfectly timed to complete this exercise safely. Depending on how large the gap is between the two roads, it's best to start signalling half way across the width of the first road. Slow down to a moderate speed.

Check the road. In a situation such as this, there is often confusion. Whether turning left or right, keep a wary eye out for cars which may misunderstand your intentions. Otherwise, things are much the same as for taking a first turning.

Steer round the corner. When turning, follow the line of the kerb, trying at all times to keep an even distance away. If you are taking a right-hand turn, you will have to enter just left of the centre line without cutting the corner.

"AT THE END OF THE ROAD TURN RIGHT PLEASE"

Where the examiner requires you to turn across a dual carriageway, it may be necessary to treat the road as if it were two separate ones, with a space to wait in the middle. If there is room for the whole of your vehicle in the safety gap in the centre it may be helpful for you to wait there. But if there is not room for you, treat it as a normal right turn and complete the movement in one go only when you can see that it is safe to do so.

What the examiner is looking for

1. Use of your mirror before signalling.
2. Correct indication in good time.
3. Good observation and control of the car, before crossing over to the central reservation without hesitation.
4. Good observation and a smooth entry on to the main road from the reservation.

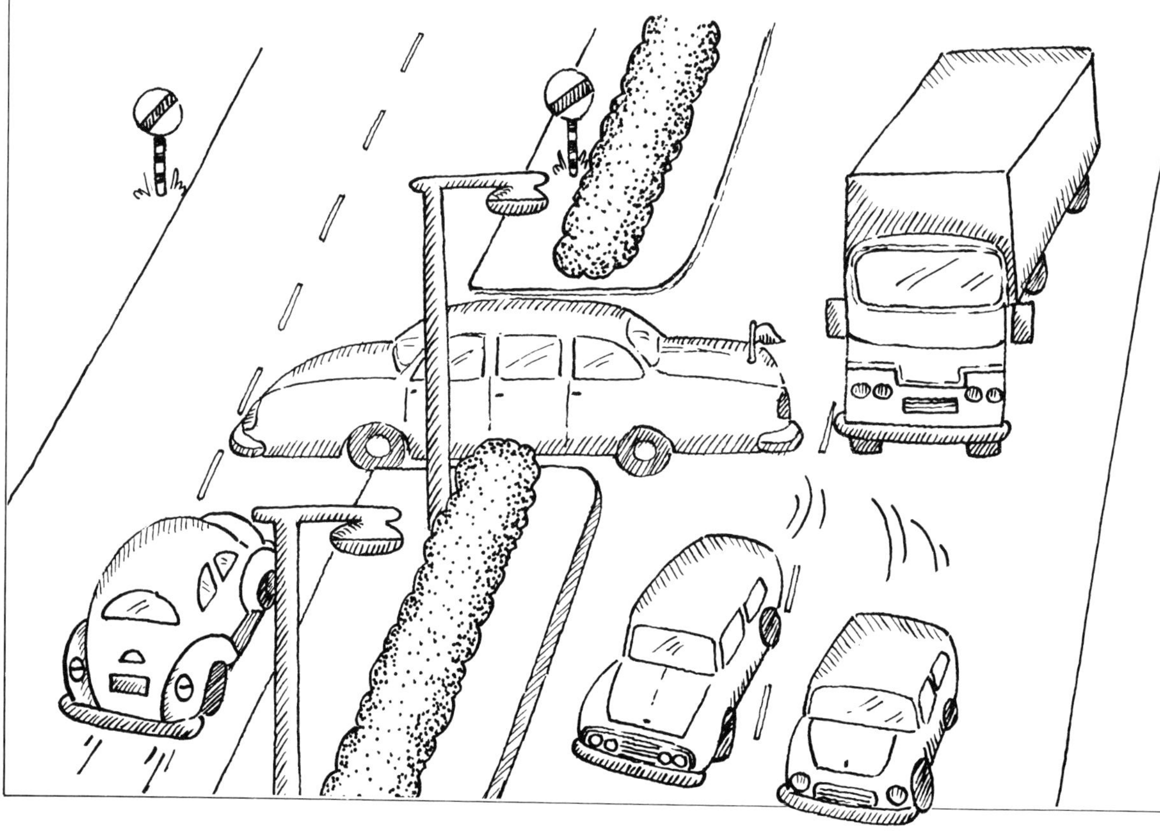

ACTION SEQUENCE

Crossing a main road with a central reservation

When crossing a fast road you must be very efficient. Never move into a central reservation unless you are certain you can wait there safely. If there is a chance that your car may stick out into a traffic lane, you must wait until you can cross the whole road before proceeding.

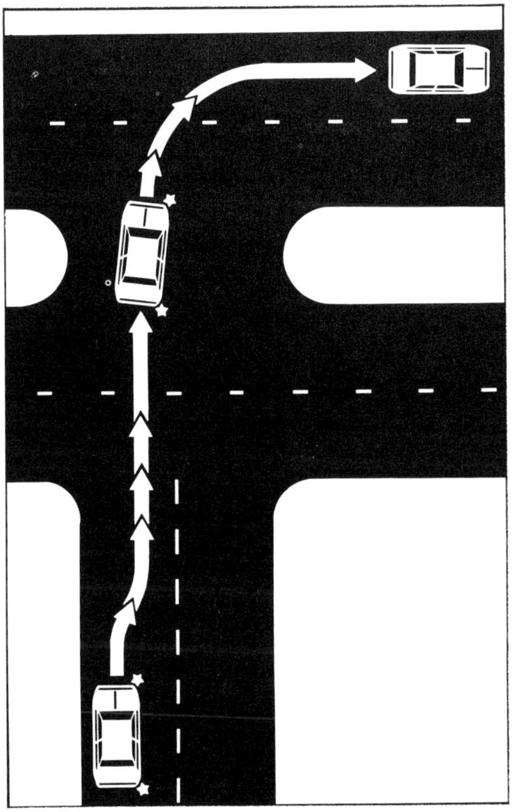

Look in your mirror. Check what's happening behind you as you approach the junction. There are likely to be two exit lanes onto a main road and you want to make sure it's safe to get into the right-hand one.

Signal, get into position and slow down. Seeing all is clear behind, indicate right and move into the right hand side or exit. Stop just short of the white lines, creeping forward if you need to see out further.

Look right to check for traffic when you reach the exit, and if it's safe to move across, do so without hesitation. Stop in the central reservation and LOOK LEFT. When there are no cars coming, move into the left hand lane. Accelerate to the appropriate speed.

"FOLLOW THE ROAD AHEAD..."

"FOLLOW THE ROAD AHEAD UNLESS I ASK YOU TO TURN"

As you approach a crossroads with the intention of continuing straight across, the examiner really need not say anything. However, should you query it or look a little confused, he would state the above.

Sometimes crossroads are strictly governed by traffic lights, sometimes by road signs and markings. In country lanes, there may be no markings, signs, lights or anything!

Great care should be taken at any crossroads, whatever the circumstances. If you have priority – meaning you're on the main road – slow down and be prepared to stop, but if your passage is clear don't hesitate! As you cross, look constantly from right to left, even into a lane where you know no traffic should be, a one-way street for example.

If you are on a minor road, crossing a main road, you must be prepared to stop before you emerge, especially if there is any doubt. But if you stop, make sure you can see when the roads will be clear. Stopping too far back could mean waiting unnecessarily.

Of course, if there is a STOP sign, you must actually stop and, momentarily at least, apply the handbrake as well.

Because traffic lights feature at so many crossroads, the Action Sequence deals specifically with them.

What the examiner is looking for

1. Good observation before signalling.

2. Correct indication in good time.

3. Regulation of speed (according to the lights) and correct positioning.

4. Handbrake on and gear disengaged if you have to stop and wait.

5. Good observation whilst on the crossroads.

ACTION SEQUENCE

Crossroad procedures

The course to take when going straight on or taking a left or right-hand turn at a crossroads is shown below.

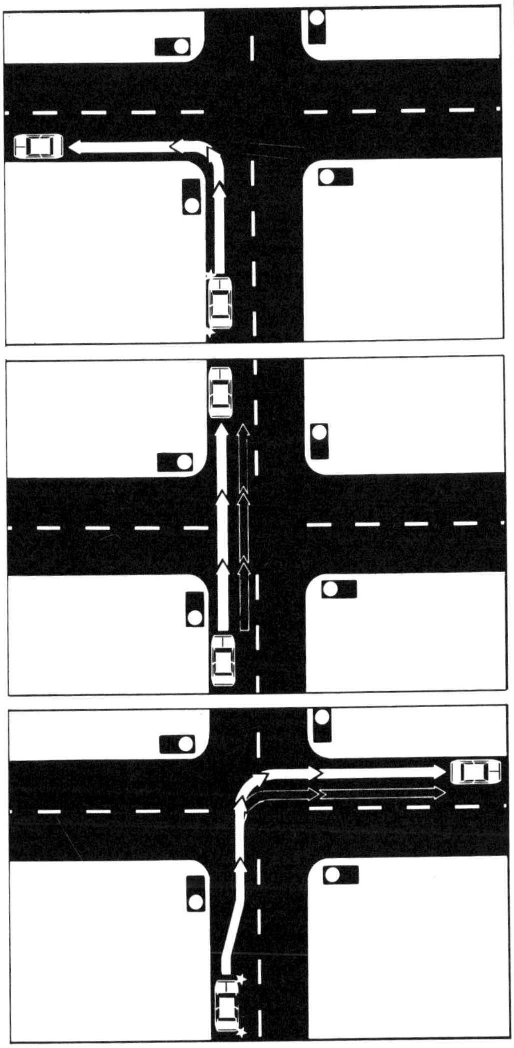

Look in your mirror. As you approach the lights, look behind to see what's happening. Also look at the road ahead: if you have a choice of lanes aim for the left hand one if turning left or going straight on and the right hand one if turning right.

Signal your intentions if you wish to turn off the main road. Indicate in good time, especially if there are lane divisions.

Get in lane and adjust your speed. Position the car correctly for your intended exit and reduce speed according to the colour of the lights. If red *or* amber is showing, slow down and stop just before the solid white line of the junction. If red *and* amber are showing slow down to a moderate speed in case you need to stop.

If you're turning off, check to see if there's a lane to 'filter off' traffic to the left or right.

Look all round. When the lights are green, and you are sure the road is clear, move off. If pedestrians are crossing the road you wish to enter, let them pass. Similarly, if turning right, allow all through traffic priority.

As you cross look from right to left. NEVER pull out into the junction if your intended exit is not clear.

"TAKE THE SECOND EXIT AT THE ROUNDABOUT"

Cars seem to come at you from all directions on a roundabout. But there are rules which normally ease the flow of traffic.

Most problems are caused by being in the wrong lane at the wrong moment, or giving the wrong signal. These problems lead to many test failures, as well as accidents. Read the Action Sequence on the facing page to check that you know the basic procedures.

When you approach a roundabout, your examiner will tell you well in advance which exit he wishes you to take.

What the examiner is looking for

1. Use of your mirror before signalling.
2. Good signalling and positioning as you approach the roundabout.
3. An approach speed consistent with traffic flow, if necessary stopping before you enter the roundabout.
4. Good observation and a smooth entry onto the roundabout.
5. Safe positioning and clear signalling on the roundabout.
6. Correct signalling as you leave the roundabout.
7. A smooth entry onto the new road and acceleration up to normal road speed.

ACTION SEQUENCE

Procedure at roundabouts with a 'two lane' entrance

At roundabouts with a 'two lane' entrance, the recommended course is shown by the white arrows, but you may follow the the black arrows if necessary. Remember that drivers already on the roundabout have priority, unless road signs dictate otherwise.

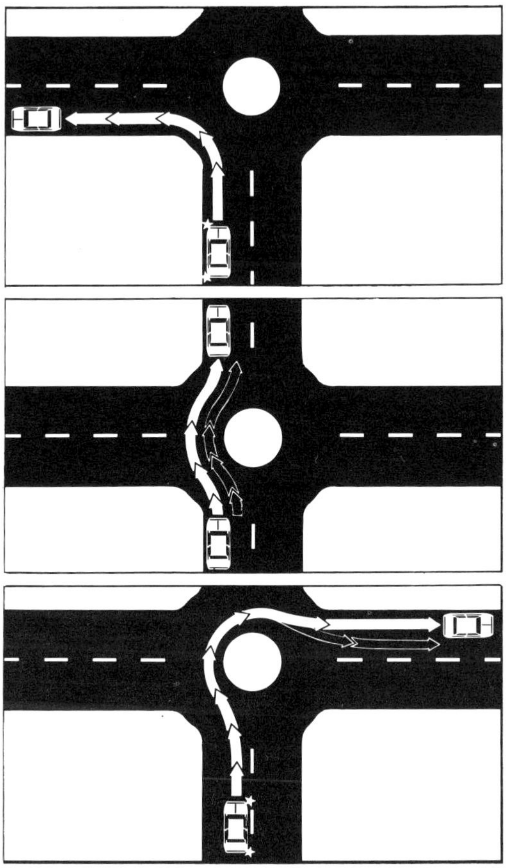

Use your mirror. Drivers behind you may change lanes unexpectedly, so keeping an eye on your rear is essential. Also, for the usual reasons, you always look behind before you use your indicator.

Signal your intentions. Drivers behind or waiting to enter the roundabout may misinterpret your next move. So on approach use your left indicator if taking the first exit, no indicator if taking the second, and the right indicator for the third exit. When on the roundabout, make sure you indicate left before you reach your exit, even when going straight on.

Get in lane. The basic rule is approach in the left-hand lane if you're turning left or going straight on. Move to the right-hand lane if you're going to take the right exit. When on the roundabout you should move to the left-hand lane just before you take your exit.

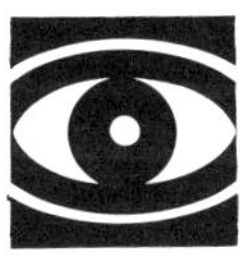

Keep a sharp look out. Remember, it is permissible to overtake on the left, so you have to watch all round. Take particular care if you change lanes when you're about to leave the roundabout.

"...SHORTLY I SHALL ASK YOU TO STOP AS IN AN EMERGENCY..."

"VERY SHORTLY I SHALL ASK YOU TO STOP AS IN AN EMERGENCY. THE SIGNAL WILL BE LIKE THIS. WHEN I DO THAT, I WANT YOU TO STOP IMMEDIATELY AND UNDER FULL CONTROL, AS THOUGH A CHILD HAD RUN OFF THE PAVEMENT."

A problem spot for most learners, the emergency stop seems to have a troublesome ring. Really it's very simple, involving a lot less than other exercises on the test. You must demonstrate total control over the car to stop very quickly. But this is all you must do. No observation, no signalling...

The examiner will warn you it's coming, and tell you which sign he'll make – generally he will slap his pad down onto the dashboard. Keep both hands on the wheel, brake firmly and progressively, and *then* check your mirror. If you were in the middle of a gear change, remember to release the clutch as you brake. Only put the clutch down just before you stop the car.

If you begin to skid, momentarily lift your foot off the brake until you feel the skid stop. Then brake again. If a skid is controlled immediately and correctly, you can still pass.

What the examiner is looking for

1. Quick, positive braking with total control.

2. No panicking.

3. Handbrake used and engine disengaged when stationary.

4. The correct pulling away procedure.

5. A smooth acceleration up to normal road speed.

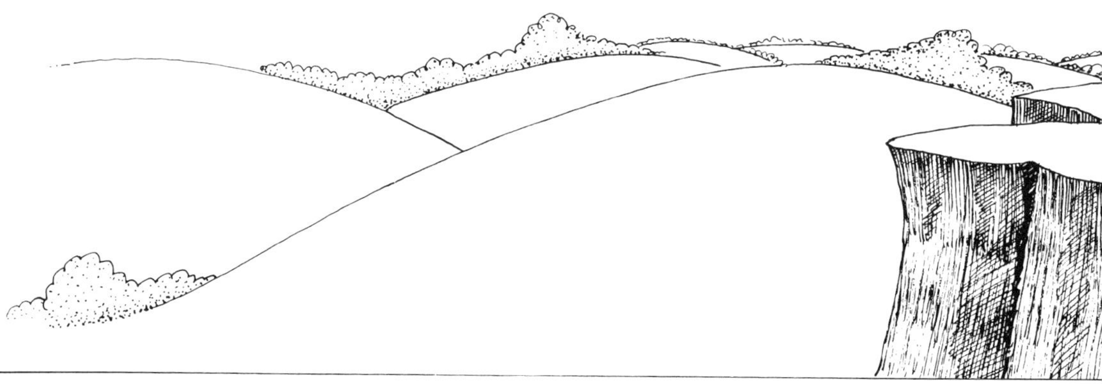

ACTION SEQUENCE

The emergency stop

No positioning or observation guidelines need to be voiced for this exercise – there are none needed! This is one of the first exercises you will be tested on, and that's because it is vital that you can simply stop your car quickly and efficiently. Don't worry if you stall – just remember your handbrake and to put your car into neutral before starting the engine.

When you have stopped, the examiner will say: "Thank you, I shall not ask you to carry out that exercise again". This is exactly what he means, and you can now rest assured that if he says the word 'stop' again during the test, he WILL NOT want you to show you can stop as in an emergency.

Brake! Brake immediately the examiner gives the signal. But don't try to do it before...! Brake firmly, and progressively. You don't need to check the mirrors first, but you should check them after you've started to brake. Keep your left foot *off* the clutch, at first, and only put the clutch down just before you stop.

Handbrake on, car in neutral. As soon as you stop, put the handbrake on and take the car out of gear. The Examiner will ask you to continue in good time.

Pull away. Look in your mirror and check your blind spots before pulling away. Accelerate up to normal road speed.

"PULL UP ON THE LEFT, AT A CONVENIENT PLACE"

When the examiner tells you to pull over, it can mean one of two things... Either he wants to tell you something (don't panic – it doesn't have to be bad news), or it's a prelude to another exercise. It's most likely to be the latter.

What the examiner is looking for

1. Use of your mirror before signalling.

2. The correct indication and a smooth reduction in speed.

3. Precise steering into a parking spot without hitting the kerb.

4. The correct precautions for a stationary vehicle, ie handbrake set and a disengaged engine.

ACTION SEQUENCE

Parking procedure

When you are asked to pull up, don't attempt squeezing yourself into a tight spot. Allow at least half-a-car's distance between yourself and other parked cars. Don't hit the kerb.

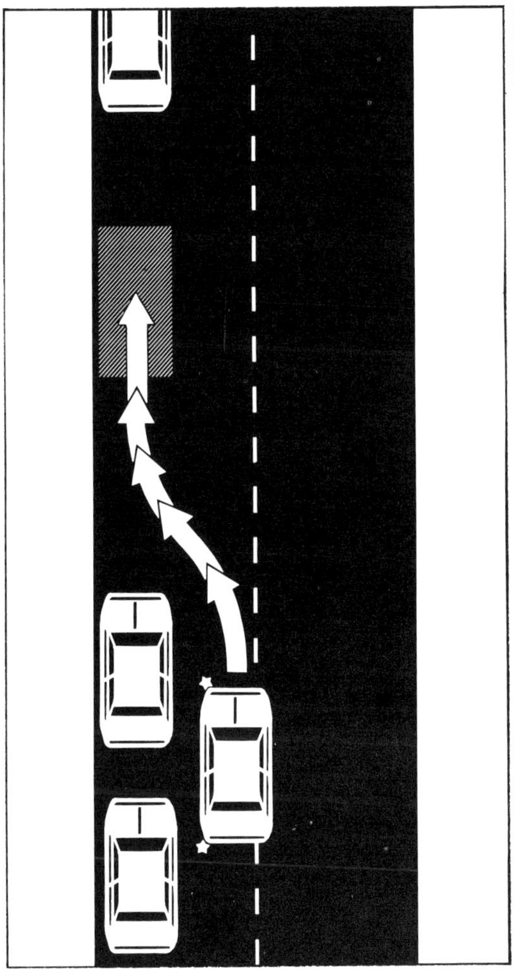

Look in your mirror. Before slowing down, consult your mirror to make sure no-one is following too close behind and that there aren't any cyclists around.

Signal to the left. Indicate left and look for a comfortable gap to pull into. The examiner will have made sure there's plenty of room for parking so it shouldn't be too tricky.

Park your car. Reduce speed and use a low gear to manoeuvre your car. Take great care not to hit the kerb, as this will count against you. Leave at least half a car's distance between yourself and any obstacle in front so pulling away won't be a problem.

Handbrake on, car in neutral. As soon as you are parked, put your handbrake on and take the car out of gear, *in that order*. Then wait for instructions. Don't turn off the engine unless the examiner asks you to do so.

"MOVE OFF WHEN YOU ARE READY..."

Moving away from a restricted parking space is called an 'angle start'. Hopefully, you'll have left enough room to pull straight out without reversing – about half a car's space in front should be enough.

Move cautiously and take extra care to check blindspots before pulling out completely.

The Action Sequence presumes your car's running and that you are strapped in and ready to drive.

What the examiner is looking for

1. Good all-round observation as you emerge from the parking spot.

2. Indication for all approaching traffic.

3. A safe exit and a smooth acceleration up to normal road speed.

ACTION SEQUENCE

Procedure for pulling away

Pulling away from a parking spot is a slow and cautious manoeuvre. Make sure your car doesn't swing out too far and, once on the road, straighten up as quickly as possible.

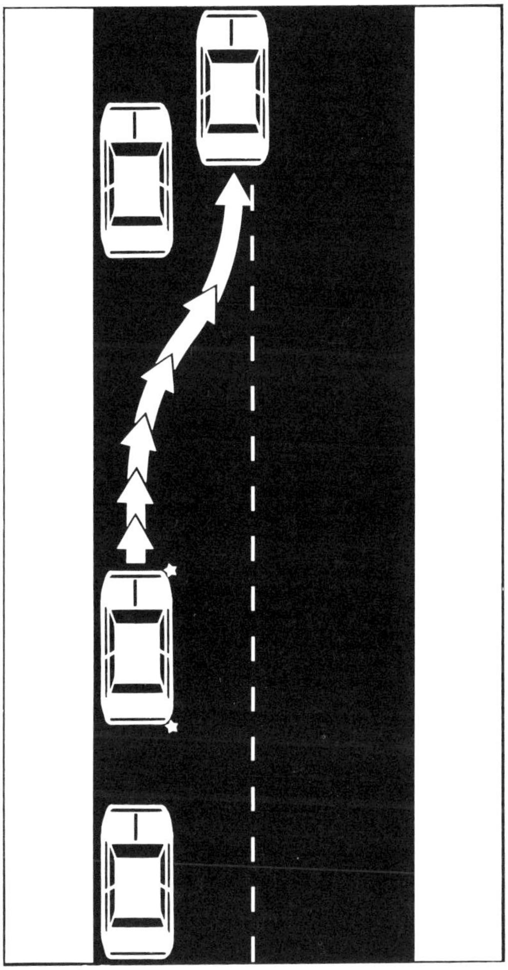

Use your mirror as a precaution. If someone is close by it might be worth putting off signalling until they've passed, to avoid causing any panic.

Signal your intentions. Indicate that you wish to pull out. If your visibility is restricted due to obstacles behind, engage first gear, let the handbrake off and creep out into the road.

Look behind. Glance over your shoulder to check all blind spots. If all is clear, pull away in an unhurried manner. If not, keep looking in the mirror, over your shoulder, and in front until you are satisfied it's safe to go.

Pull away. If you haven't already done so, engage first gear, bring your clutch to 'biting point' and release your handbrake. Look behind as much as necessary, but don't neglect the road ahead. When all is safe and clear, pull smoothly away.

HILL START – UP

"MOVE OFF WHEN YOU ARE READY..."

Most exercises test your basic driving ability and road knowledge, but some are more specific.

The hill start demands complete control. Pulling away without slipping back or overworking your engine isn't easy. But it's what you must do. And you still have to show all the correct observation.

Don't be fooled into false security on a minor slope – you're just as likely to roll back. You need slightly more revs than usual to get going up the hill, but don't let this result in either a jerky start or a wheelspin getaway – careful control of the clutch, handbrake and accelerator will prevent these things from happening.

What the examiner is looking for

1. Good observation, especially of the blind spot.

2. Signalling if necessary.

3. A smooth and safe entry onto the road, without slipping backwards or causing excessive engine noise.

4. A gentle increase up to normal road speed.

ACTION SEQUENCE

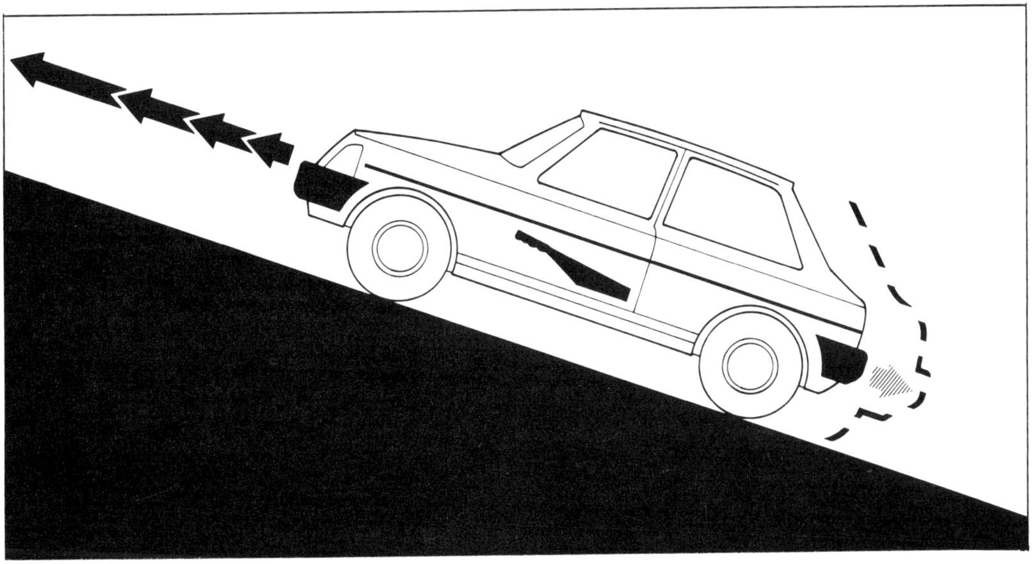

Pulling away up a hill

The actual manoeuvring involved in a hill start is minimal, especially as the examiner will never ask you to do this exercise from a restricted parking position. However, good control of your clutch and handbrake is essential if no rolling is to take place.

Check behind before moving off. Look in your mirror and also turn round to check any blind spots. Although your mirror gives a fair back view, it's essential you check any hidden corners. There could be a slow-moving cyclist approaching, for example, who could easily be missed from a glance at your mirror alone.

Signal if necessary. If the road you're moving into is completely clear of traffic, there's no need to indicate. If a car is approaching in the distance, signal right to indicate your intention.

Look again and pull away. Engage first gear, increase your engine revs to biting point and release the handbrake. With a quick check in your mirror and another glance behind, begin to pull away. Keep the revs coming to ensure a smooth pull out into the road. And don't try to change into second gear too soon.

HILL START – DOWN

"MOVE OFF WHEN YOU ARE READY..."

Examiners don't often ask you to do a downhill start. If they do, the reason may be to check your ability to fully control the car while gravity encourages run-away speed. Never, never freewheel when starting or stopping on a downhill slope. (Freewheeling is letting the car roll while out of gear or while the clutch is down.) If you do it will count against you because you have allowed the car to get 'out of control'.

What the examiner is looking for

1. Good observation before indicating.

2. An indication to any approaching traffic.

3. A smooth entry onto the road, making sure the engine is constantly engaged and there's no freewheeling.

4. A steady increase to normal road speed.

ACTION SEQUENCE

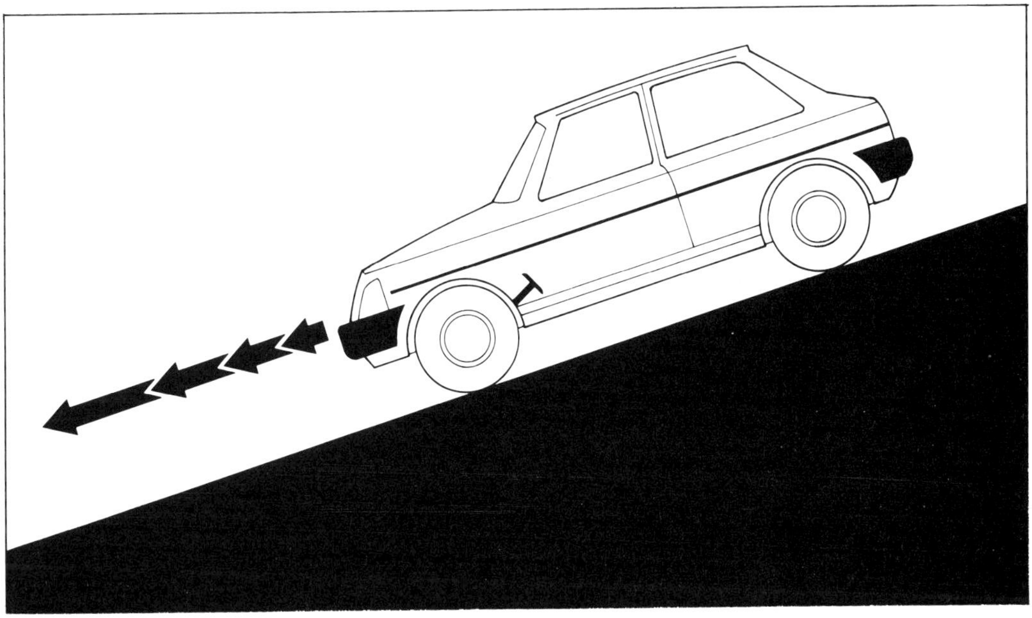

Pulling away down a hill

As with an uphill start, the positioning and manoeuvring of your vehicle is straightforward. Control of the engine and good use of your footbrake is what's being tested.

Check behind. Use your mirror to see if anything is coming. When it looks clear to go, look over your shoulder to double-check.

Signal if necessary. Your indicator is to tell other drivers and road users what you are doing. If, looking round, you find there is no traffic approaching, you are not obliged to use it. However, if there's a bend or turning where traffic is likely to appear, it is advisable to indicate anyway.

Look again and pull away. The temptation to roll is enormous, but don't. Select first or second gear, according to the steepness of the hill, press the footbrake firmly, release the handbrake; reach biting point with the clutch and then slowly release the footbrake and put your right foot onto the accelerator pedal.

Keep checking behind, with quick glances over your shoulder, as you emerge.

REVERSING TO THE LEFT

"...I SHOULD LIKE YOU TO REVERSE..."

"THE ROAD ON THE LEFT IS THE ONE I SHOULD LIKE YOU TO REVERSE INTO. DRIVE PAST IT AND STOP. THEN BACK IN AND CONTINUE TO DRIVE IN REVERSE GEAR FOR SOME DISTANCE, KEEPING REASONABLY CLOSE TO THE KERB."

It's obvious what's being tested in this exercise: your precision in reversing. The examiner will probably get you to pull over just before the exit he wants you to reverse into. He'll explain what you have to do. You'll then have to reposition yourself the correct side of the corner. Make sure you don't forget the correct precautions for pulling in and out (see pages 48-51). There are a number of points to remember when reversing.

- You can remove your seat belt for this exercise. But DO remember to replace it afterwards.
- If you think you're going off-line, it won't count against you if you stop, go forward and reposition yourself.
- You don't have to indicate, it only confuses other drivers.

What the examiner is looking for

1. Look all round before moving. Cautious observation to the front and back throughout the exercise. Especially important are the full look round to the front, immediately prior to turning the wheels and a careful look through the back window as you reverse down the road.

2. Steady control of the clutch.

3. Precise steering round the corner – without hitting the kerb or swinging too wide of the corner.

4. Safety precautions once you've finished – handbrake on, car in neutral.

ACTION SEQUENCE

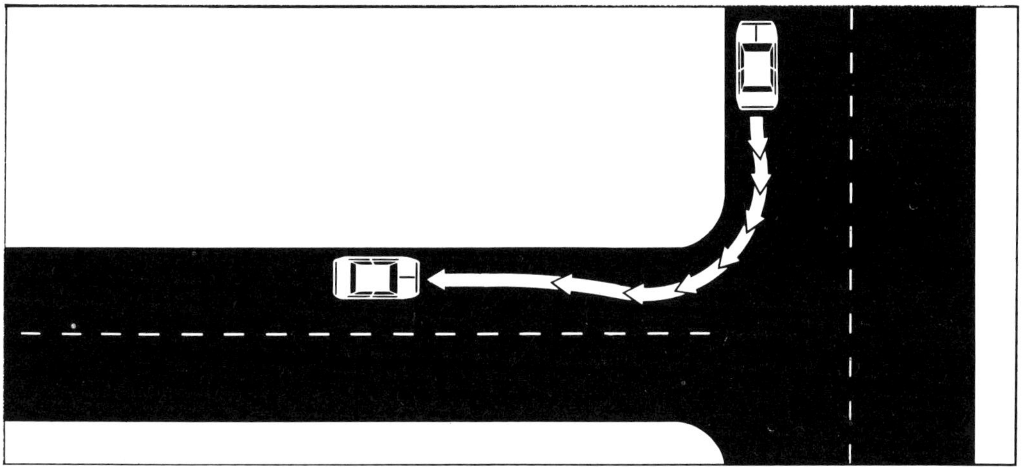

Reversing round a left-hand corner

This is probably one of the most awkward manoeuvres of the test. Follow the line of the kerb as much as possible and try not to swing out whilst turning. Go back a fair distance once you are round the corner so the examiner can judge your ability to reverse in a straight line.

Pull up. Showing all the usual caution (see page 50), position yourself just past the corner you are to reverse round. Remember, if you go too far it will only mean more work!

Look all round. Use your mirror and look all round before moving. There could easily be pedestrians crossing or walking around your car.

Reverse round the corner. Engage reverse gear and begin moving back slowly and steadily – there's no bonus for hurrying! As you reach the turning, check the road you are leaving, as well as the one you're entering. Remember, the front of your car will swing out as you go round.

Once round the corner, reverse in a straight line for several car spaces, looking out of the back window as you go. If you don't reverse far enough, the examiner will ask you to continue.

Handbrake on, car in neutral. When you stop, put your handbrake on and take the car out of gear. Replace your seat belt if it was removed.

REVERSING TO THE RIGHT

"...I SHOULD LIKE YOU TO REVERSE..."

**"THE ROAD ON THE RIGHT IS THE ONE I SHOULD LIKE YOU TO REVERSE INTO.
DRIVE PAST IT AND STOP. THEN BACK IN AND CONTINUE TO DRIVE IN REVERSE GEAR FOR SOME DISTANCE, KEEPING REASONABLY CLOSE TO THE KERB."**

It's rare to have to reverse right around a corner. The exercise is usually reserved for trucks and vans where side vision is restricted. But just in case this applies to you...

The examiner will ask you to pull up before the exercise and explain what he wants. Then you'll have to cross over the road to get into position. Show great care as you do this. Throughout the exercise, you are going to be an obstacle for other traffic. And your view will be limited and virtually blind in places. Because of this, it is vitally important that you look all round to ensure the road is clear behind and around you. This will mean looking through the side windows, to the front, and through whatever mirrors are available.

What the examiner is looking for

1. A thorough check all round your car before moving and throughout the exercise, paying special attention to any blind areas.

2. Good control of the clutch.

3. Precise steering without hitting the kerb. A higher standard would be expected than on the left hand turn, as your visibility of the corner itself is greatly improved.

4. The handbrake on and car put into neutral. Also, seat belt replaced if removed.

ACTION SEQUENCE

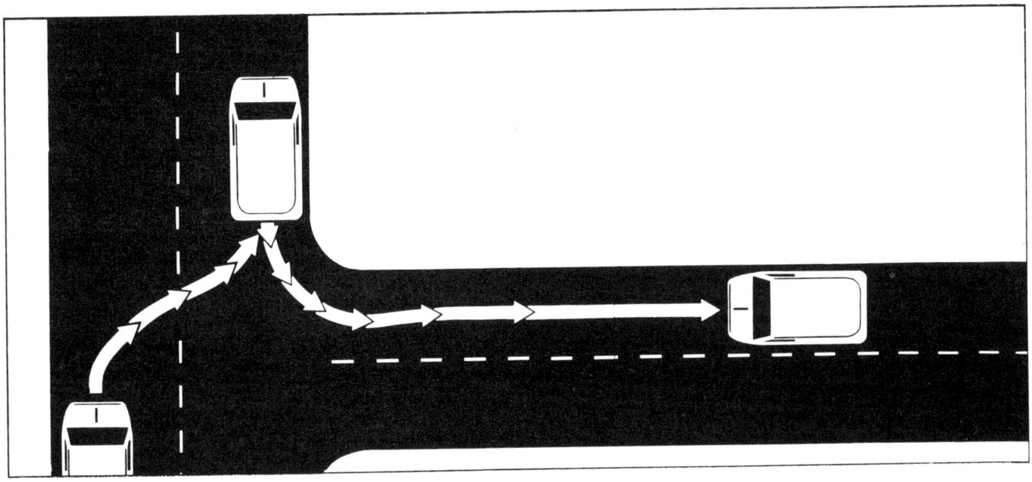

Reversing round a right-hand corner

If you take your test in a van or small lorry your reversing is likely to be tested on a right-hand corner, as opposed to a left. If so, your positioning will be expected to be near perfect. Observation is more likely to be the stumbling block.

Pull up. Once you've crossed over the road, pull up just beyond the corner. Naturally you mustn't hinder anyone's access but, within reason, get as close to the corner as possible.

Look all round the front and back of your vehicle. Be particularly wary of pedestrians who may be crossing the road.

Reverse around the corner. Engage reverse gear and move slowly and steadily. Keeping on course should be easy. But do keep looking out, especially when the front of your car swings out during your turn. Once around the corner, keep steadily reversing until you are well clear of the junction – a length of six or seven cars is about right. This will be safe for other cars, and give you enough room to pull out and across to the correct side of the road.

Handbrake on, car in neutral. Once you've stopped, apply the handbrake *before* taking the car out of gear. Also, replace your belt if it was removed during the exercise to make observation easier.

"I'D LIKE YOU TO TURN YOUR CAR..."

"I'D LIKE YOU TO TURN YOUR CAR ROUND IN THE ROAD, TO FACE THE OPPOSITE DIRECTION, USING FORWARD AND REVERSE GEARS. TRY NOT TO TOUCH THE KERB WHEN YOU ARE TURNING."

You may be confused by this long-winded instruction. What the examiner wants is a simple three-point turn! Ohhh...why didn't he say so? Perhaps because it's misleading: you don't have to do a three-point turn, but can take as many as seven moves (or even more!), depending on the size of your car and the width of the road.

This exercise demands good control of the clutch and precise steering. You must also show the strictest observation, looking left and right after each separate movement and behind when applicable. Hopefully the road will remain clear throughout. But if a car approaches while you're halfway through, don't panic. You must sit, wait, and most importantly *watch*. Don't move another inch until you're sure of the other car's decision, either to wait or to pass cautiously by.

Don't give any signals – indicating is not necessary except at the beginning, when you pull up.

What the examiner is looking for

1. Good observation at each stopping point of the turn, and throughout the exercise.

2. Accurate steering, avoiding the kerb and showing good judgement of where the front and back of your car are.

3. Good control of the clutch.

4. Your handbrake used and the gear disengaged at each stopping point.

5. A smooth acceleration up to normal road speed on completion of the turn.

ACTION SEQUENCE

Turning your car around

Below you can see the turning angles required for a three-point turn. Always stop short of the kerb, and don't be afraid to use more moves to complete the exercise.

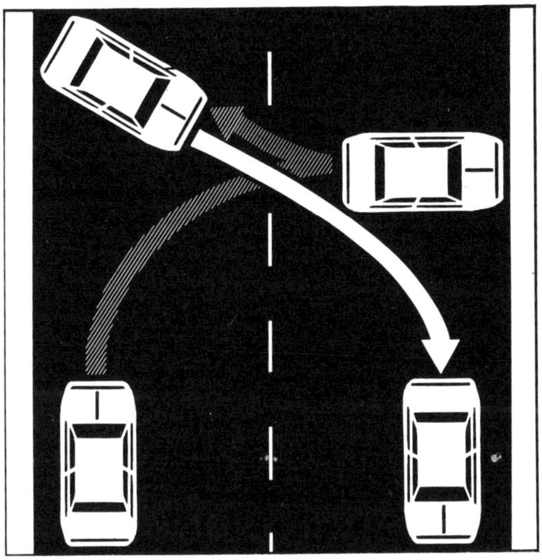

Pull over. Once you're asked to pull over for this exercise, it's best to get fairly close to the kerb (don't hit it though!). This way you have more room for the manoeuvre itself. Wait with the handbrake on and the engine disengaged.

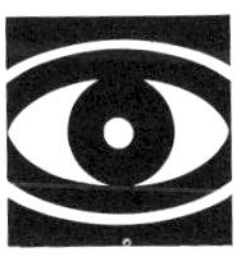

Look all round. The examiner will have planned a quiet road, but you must wait until it's absolutely clear before you begin. Look in front and behind. Make sure there are no children nearby, especially in your blind spots.

Steer across the road. The road is clear. Engage first gear, take the handbrake off and steer across the road, as shown in the diagram. About two-thirds of the way across, begin to straighten up. Remember to pass the wheel from hand to hand (at the ten to two, or quarter to three position). Stop just before the kerb.

Handbrake on, look all round. Having reached the other side of the road, put your handbrake on and select neutral. Look in both traffic directions and behind, where pedestrians may lurk. If all is clear, engage reverse gear and release the handbrake.

Reverse back across the road by turning your steering wheel to the left and constantly checking all around. Stop as you near the kerb.

Handbrake on, look all round. Put your handbrake back on, and take the car out of reverse. Check the way is clear to pull out.

Steer into the left hand lane. Engage first gear and, letting the handbrake off, turn the wheel fully to the right until you are able to take up a normal driving position. Sometimes the examiner will tell you to continue driving. But if you removed your seat belt, stop and replace it.

"...I SHOULD NOW LIKE TO ASK YOU SOME QUESTIONS..."

"THAT CONCLUDES THE PRACTICAL PART OF THE TEST, I SHOULD NOW LIKE TO ASK YOU SOME QUESTIONS ON THE HIGHWAY CODE AND OTHER MOTORING MATTERS."

The test is now nearly at an end. You have finished the practical part of the test, and all that remains are the questions on the Highway Code.

You will be asked about five questions and shown six traffic signs to identify. Questions on motorways could prove to be the most difficult as you have no practical experience of them. But if you go through the Highway Code book with your instructor beforehand, nothing should give you too many problems.

The examiner will not tell you whether the answers you give are correct or not. He will simply say "I see" or "Thank you".

Although it is possible to fail the driving test on the Highway Code questions alone, this is most unlikely.

Here's a selection of questions the examiner may ask, and the answers he would expect in each case.

What is the name given to the extra lane for the purpose of slowing down prior to leaving a motorway?
The deceleration lane.

What is the correct changing sequence of traffic lights?
Red, red and amber, green, amber, red.

When are you allowed to overtake on the left?
When the car in front is turning to the right and you can pass on the left without getting in the way of others. At a roundabout. When right lane traffic in a two-lane road is moving slower than the left in slow-moving traffic. In a one-way system. A tramcar, except when stationary.

Where must you not reverse your vehicle?
From a side road into a main road.

What is the first thing you must do if involved in an accident?
Stop.

What white lines are painted on the road at a 'stop' sign?
One solid white line.

Where do you see yellow zig-zag markings?
Entrances or lengths of road that must be kept clear.

What particular danger is there when you are turning left?
Cyclists and motorcyclists coming up from behind on the left hand side. And pedestrians crossing the road you wish to enter.

When should you use your horn?
When it is necessary to warn other road users of your presence on the road.

"...I'M PLEASED TO TELL YOU THAT YOU HAVE PASSED..."

"THAT IS THE END OF THE TEST, AND I'M PLEASED TO TELL YOU THAT YOU HAVE PASSED. WILL YOU SIGN HERE ON THIS PASS CERTIFICATE PLEASE."

It's about this time that the examiner comes out from behind his official mask and smiles.

He asks you to confirm your address hasn't changed. Then he will want to see your licence.

He will ask you to sign the pass certificate, then give it, or a copy, for you to send off to the DVLC with your provisional licence ... You've passed!

The last thing you want from this glorious occasion is an overdose of confidence. Having passed your test, the real task of learning to drive on your own is just about to start.

Any honest driver will admit that new situations crop up with incredible regularity, and that driving is a continuous lesson. So, rather than a certificate of competence, think of your pass as a licence for you to continue to learn.

"...I'M SORRY YOU HAVEN'T PASSED..."

"THAT'S THE END OF THE TEST, I'M SORRY YOU HAVEN'T PASSED, BUT YOUR DRIVING HAS NOT REACHED THE REQUIRED STANDARD. IF YOU GIVE ME A FEW MOMENTS I'LL HELP YOU BY MARKING THE POINTS TO WHICH YOU SHOULD GIVE SPECIAL ATTENTION."

You didn't pass. Oh well, it is not the end of the world, and now is the time to plan your next test. Discuss the failure form (DL 24) which the examiner will have marked for you with your instructor. On it you will find that he has underlined only those items which were actually dangerous or potentially so. These are the items you should pay particular attention to before your next test. But don't neglect everything else. The fact that some items have not been underlined does not mean they were done perfectly, only that those errors would have been minor ones. And minor mistakes of any kind will not fail you.

Look at the 'Statement of Failure' form as a consolation prize, awarded to those who attended but could not pass this time.

The examiner is not allowed to discuss the errors you made, partly because of the time factor, but mainly because it avoids any arguments.

A good instructor will be able to take you out, test you, and produce the same sort of report on your driving as the examiner did. If you took a test without using an instructor, perhaps now is the time you should seriously think about looking for a good one.

If you were to fail your test, the examiner would supply you with a failure form like the one opposite. This form lists all the points being tested by the driving test, from the individual exercises explained in this book to the general safety requirements that every driver should know.
The candidate shown here has failed to pass because of item number 13 "Make progress by / driving at a speed appropriate to the road and traffic conditions / avoiding undue hesitancy".
In this particular case only the words "Make progress by avoiding undue hesitancy" have been underlined, explaining that the cause of failure in this instance was due to this, rather than driving too slowly.
The candidate clearly hesitated and waited at a place on the road where it would have been safer to have kept going. Perhaps the candidate was too far back in the mouth of a junction and could not see if the road was clear or busy.

Department of Transport

ROAD TRAFFIC ACT 1972

Test Centre

Statement of Failure to Pass Test of Competence to Drive

Name ..A.N. Other..

has this day been examined and has failed to pass the test of competence to drive prescribed for the purposes of section 85 of the Road Traffic Act 1972.

Date ..1st April 1984..

Authorised by the Secretary of State to conduct tests

Examiners have regard to the items listed below in deciding whether a candidate is competent to drive. The matters needing special attention are marked for your information and assistance and should be studied in detail. (See Note 1 overleaf)

1. ☐ Comply with the requirements of the eyesight test.
2. ☐ Know the Highway Code.
3. ☐ Take proper precautions before starting the engine.
4. ☐ Make proper use of/accelerator/clutch/gears/footbrake/handbrake/steering.
5. ☐ Move away/safely/under control.
6. ☐ Stop the vehicle in an emergency/promptly/under control/making proper use of front brake.
7. ☐ Reverse into a limited opening either to the right or left/under control/with due regard for other road users.
8. ☐ Turn round by means of forward and reverse gears/under control/with due regard for other road users.
9. ☐ Make effective use of mirror(s) well before / Take effective rear observation well before } signalling/changing direction/slowing down or stopping.
10. ☐ Give signals/where necessary/correctly/in good time.
11. ☐ Take prompt and appropriate action on all/traffic signs/road markings/traffic lights/signals given by traffic controllers/other road users.
12. ☐ Exercise proper care in the use of speed.
13. ☒ Make progress by/driving at a speed appropriate to the road and traffic conditions/avoiding undue hesitancy.
14. ☐ Act properly at road junctions:–
    - regulate speed correctly on approach;
    - take effective observation before emerging;
    - position the vehicle correctly/before turning right/before turning left;
    - avoid cutting right hand corners.
15. ☐ Overtake/meet/cross the path of/other vehicles safely.
16. ☐ Position the vehicle correctly during normal driving.
17. ☐ Allow adequate clearance to stationary vehicles.
18. ☐ Take appropriate action at pedestrian crossings.
19. ☐ Select a safe position for normal stops.
20. ☐ Show awareness and anticipation of the actions of/pedestrians/cyclists/drivers.

DRIVING EXAMINERS ARE NOT PERMITTED TO DISCUSS DETAILS OF THE TEST

SEE GUIDANCE NOTES OVERLEAF

Printed in the UK for H.M.S.O., Dd 8300589, 3/84, (GP 33489/9).

DL24
9/81

ROAD WORKS
PASS FIRST TIME

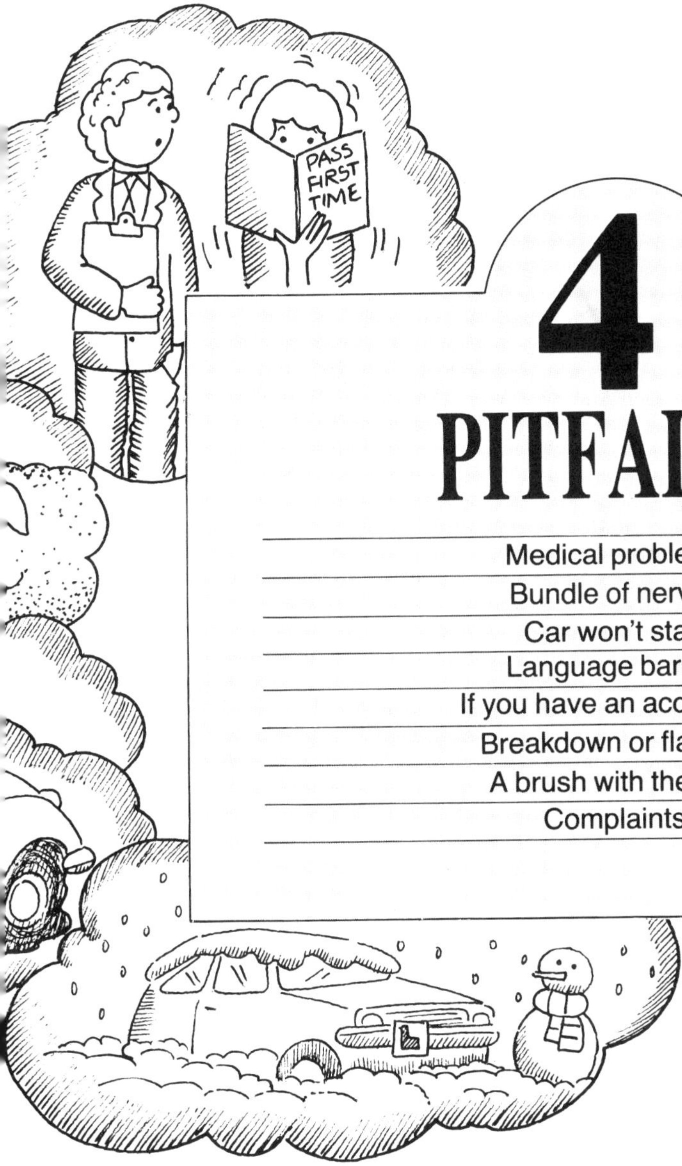

4 PITFALLS

MEDICAL PROBLEMS

If you are deaf, or deaf and mute, then it is important that you explain this fact on a sheet of paper attached to your test application. The examiner who takes you out will have been carefully selected because of his interest and care for your particular problems.

The only other medical condition that seems to cause problems is pregnancy... Often the first few months of pregnancy are accompanied by fainting fits and dizzy spells. If this is the case with you, postpone the test. Usually these problems will disappear and then you can confidently take your test – so long as you can fit behind the steering wheel and still reach the pedals!

BUNDLE OF NERVES

Virtually everyone suffers from nerves during their test. For many people this may not be a bad thing because it improves their concentration. Others may react differently. A bad case of nerves can leave some people incapable of anything. If you fear this may happen to you, pay a visit to your doctor. He may be able to advise you on relaxation techniques, or suggest something to take that will help to calm you down. Besides this, it's worth making practice runs with different co-drivers so you get used to having someone other than your usual partner with you.

Examiners are normally tolerant of test 'nerves', but if your driving is badly affected he will have no choice but to fail you.

CAR WON'T START

Imagine trying to begin your test and finding your engine won't start. It's enough to make you weep. If you've already driven the car to the test centre, however, the problem is unlikely to be serious. The two most likely causes are:

- An air lock in the fuel system. To remedy this, give a long, steady burst on the accelerator pedal on turning the key. This should clear the air lock and allow the engine to catch. Don't pump the pedal though, as this could flood the carburettor and make matters worse.
- If absolutely nothing happens when you try to start, the problem is likely to be electrical – maybe a blown fuse or loose battery connection. Take a quick look and, if this is the case, it should be easy to reconnect wires or replace a fuse.

That said, if you have any doubts over the fitness of your car, check it thoroughly BEFORE the test. Check obvious things like the battery connections, fuses etc. (see page 12). The examiner will tolerate a small amount of tinkering, but not a lot, before abandoning the test. Alternatively, borrow someone else's car, or use your instructor's.

LANGUAGE BARRIER

If you, or someone you know, wishes to take a test in this country but can't speak the language, there's a simple solution. Arrange for an interpreter to sit the test with you. Test centres don't supply interpreters but they will allow one to accompany you throughout the test. Remember that he is only there to interpret and must not assist you in any other way. Remember also that you must be able to read and understand all traffic signals.

IF YOU HAVE AN ACCIDENT...

In the event of an accident, remember that you are in charge. The examiner is only an observer. Move your car out of the way of other traffic and then exchange details with the other party involved. You both need each other's address, car registration number and insurance company's name and address, and that of the vehicle's owner if different from that of the driver.

If you do have an accident, the examiner must be sure in his own mind that you are in a fit state to continue. If he is not sure he will abandon the test. Whether you will fail, or have the test abandoned and be told to ask for a new one depends upon the circumstances of the accident. For a more detailed account of the accident procedures you should follow, see page 79.

BREAKDOWN OR FLAT TYRE

If your car breaks down during the test, this means trouble. The examiner may give you a few minutes to locate and cure the problem, but unless quickly remedied, the test will be abandoned. However, it isn't all bad: you won't have to wait the usual month for your next test date as you won't have failed.

If you have a flat tyre similar rules apply. Unless you are almost at the end of your test, and the examiner feels that he has been able to give you a fair assessment, the test will be abandoned. Even for an experienced driver, it normally takes about ten minutes to change a wheel, and that time would be too much for an examiner to spare on your test.

A BRUSH WITH THE LAW

If your car is obviously roadworthy and taxed, and your driving competent, you are unlikely to be stopped by the police. But if you are, don't panic. The police are generally very tolerant with learner drivers. Nevertheless, exceeding a speed limit or ignoring traffic signals of any kind is an offence as well as a likely cause of test failure. For more advice about driving and the law read Section 5.

COMPLAINTS

There is no way in which a driving test decision can be reversed, but if you feel that the examiner did not conduct the test fairly, or that it was not in accordance with the rules, you are allowed to go before a magistrate's court to ask for a re-test. But your evidence must be pretty good. You would have to prove that the examiner was drunk, or acted out of malice or some similar malpractice, to win your case.

POLICE
COP 1
MAD 001

5
RULES OF THE ROAD

The law and your car

Driving and the law

Fines and endorsements

Drink and driving

Reckless driving

Accident procedures

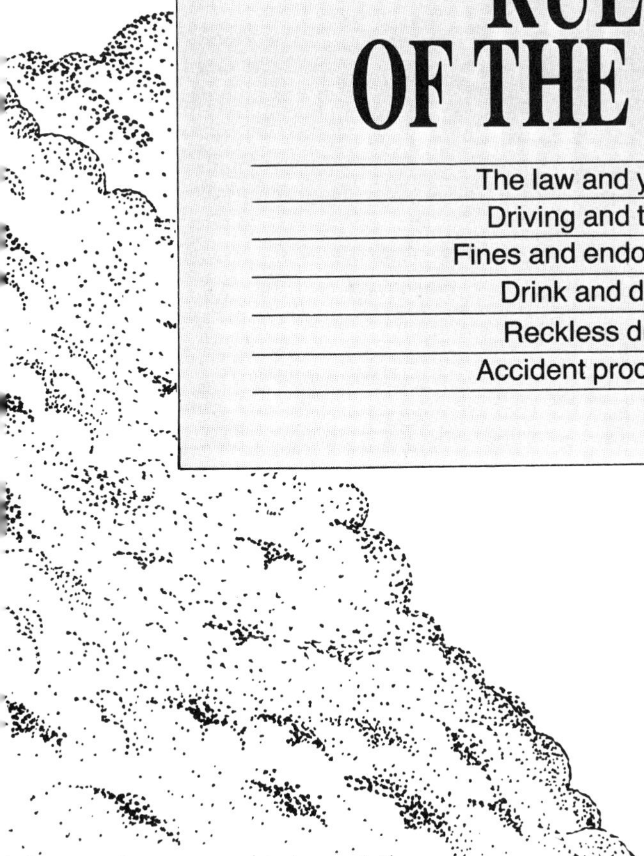

Once you've passed your test, don't forget the fact that it is easier to lose your licence than it is to gain it. This last section, therefore, covers the laws of the road and shows just how easily you can lose your right to drive. Reading the Highway Code is a must for any learner driver since it not only explains about traffic signs, rules and procedures, but also outlines all the basic laws that relate to motoring. Copies can be obtained for a moderate price from most bookshops or direct from Her Majesty's Stationary Office.

THE LAW AND YOUR CAR

Owning and driving a car means you have a responsibility to ensure its safety on the roads. Three documents (excluding the registration document or 'log book' which states the ownership and basic details of the car) have to be obtained: an insurance certificate, a tax disc and an MOT certificate.

Insurance certificate. Insurance is vital. The cover you get for the car itself can vary, but remember more importantly that motor insurance is there for those who may issue claims against you, especially pedestrians or other injured parties. Make sure you understand the conditions of your policy and *when*, *where* and *who* it covers. The premium you pay, having just passed your test, may be rather high, but with years of careful driving it can be reduced.

The minimum insurance you are required to have *by law* is called Third Party Personal Injury cover. This means you are covered if someone makes a claim against you in the event of an accident. This level of cover, however, means the insurance company would not pay for any damage to your car – unless it can be proved that it was the other driver's fault. And if this was the case, they would claim off the other driver's insurers.

Many people choose to add 'Fire and Theft' cover to the basic Third Party policy. This way, your car is insured against both these risks as well.

Comprehensive cover is another alternative. This covers you against any third party claim, and also covers any damage that your car may suffer. It is expensive, but the premiums can be reduced by, for example, restricting the policy to just one or two named drivers or by agreeing to pay an 'excess' of the first £50 or £100 of any claim.

Premiums on all policies are reduced by a 'No Claims Bonus'. This knocks a percentage off the premium for each year you don't make a claim. Savings of 60% or so can build up after 5 years' trouble-free motoring.

MOT certificate. The MOT certificate is to confirm that your car is in a roadworthy condition and complies with legal requirements. (It's never recommended to buy a vehicle without one.) All vehicles that have passed their third birthday need a current certificate, otherwise the driver is liable to a maximum £100 fine. However, even when you hold a current MOT, your car must be properly maintained to keep it on the right side of the law. Some of the points to watch out for are:

Brakes and steering. Your foot and hand brakes are likely to need adjusting throughout the year. And both brake and steering parts are likely to wear. If you're not confident about maintaining these yourself, put your car in for a regular service (every 6 months is usual), rather than neglecting them. They are the most important safety functions of your car.

Tyres. Tyre pressure and condition should be checked regularly (each week). Less than 1 mm of tread on three-quarters of a tyre's surface, or lumps, ridges and splits, mean the tyre needs replacing. Don't put off having a worn tyre changed – the fines are huge.

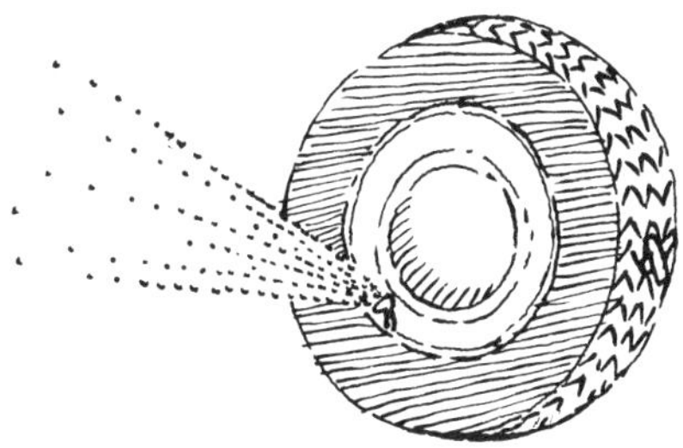

Exhaust system. If your exhaust begins blowing, either seal up the damaged area or have the system replaced. A maximum £100 fine can be imposed for driving an excessively noisy vehicle.

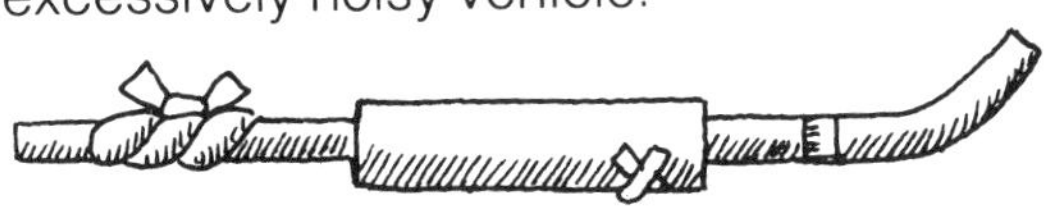

Lights. Headlights, side, rear and brake lights, indicators and hazard warning lights (if applicable) must be working at all times.

Ancillary equipment. Horn, speedometer, seatbelts, mirrors and windscreen washers and wipers each have an important purpose. Ensure that all are kept clean and in working order.

Road tax. Having acquired your insurance, and being in possession of an MOT certificate, you need to tax your vehicle. Whether a car is in use or not, if it sits on a public highway it is liable for road tax. This is not for safety reasons, but is simply a levy on all car owners for use of the roads. To get your tax disc you must take your registration document, MOT and insurance certificates to the Post Office. Ask for form V10 and fill it in. Charges vary depending on the class of vehicle and term you wish to opt for (6 months or a year), but for a private car the cost is currently £100 per annum.

All three documents will need periodic renewal so keep tabs on them. Reminders are sent through the post in the case of insurance and tax, but the MOT is wholly your responsibility. A new certificate can be applied for up to a month before the expiry date of the old.

If all the mentioned parts of your car are checked and corrected accordingly on a regular basis, and an MOT certificate, insurance certificate, and tax disc are continually in operation, then you can be fairly certain that your car is both safe and legal.

DRIVING AND THE LAW

Just as the law demands things of your car, it also makes demands on you, the driver. Naturally, you must possess a licence and this must cover you for the class of vehicle you wish to drive. On passing your test and receiving your full licence, make sure you sign it – believe it or not, an unsigned licence is an offence. Your eyesight must be adequate so if you wear glasses or contact lenses, never drive without them.

Many of the laws of the road are mentioned in Section 2 of this book as general driving tips, but just to impress upon you that they are *laws* and must be *obeyed*, here's a summary of important do's and don'ts:

- Do wear a seat belt at all times and ensure that any front seat passenger does the same.
- Do obey all road signs and markings, especially speed limits and parking restrictions.
- Do park in the direction of the traffic flow at night – reflectors at the rear of your car warn drivers it is there. And if you park in an unlit road where speeds of over 30 mph are permissible, do leave your parking lights on, unless your car is in a recognised parking place.
- Do give pedestrians precedence at all crossings.
- Do obey signals given by the police, traffic wardens and School Crossing Patrols.
- Do always turn off the engine before you leave the vehicle (and apply your handbrake).
- Don't drive recklessly or without care and attention (also see page 79).
- Don't drive or park in bus lanes during their hours of operation.
- Don't drive under the influence of drink or drugs (see page 78).
- Don't carry an excessive number of passengers. Not only does this make a mockery of the concentration that driving requires, it can also invalidate your insurance.
- Don't use your horn during prohibited hours (11.30pm – 7.00am) or when stationary, unless to prevent an accident.
- Don't dazzle drivers with your headlights or fog lamps, and never use fog lamps unless *severe* weather conditions dictate.
- Don't use hazard lights whilst moving.
- Don't park closer than 15 yards away from a junction.
- Don't open your door on pedestrians.
- Don't park anywhere where signs dictate otherwise, or where you are obstructing other vehicles, entrances, pavements, pedestrian crossings, or where you could cause danger.
- Don't drive a vehicle unsuitable for your size that you cannot sit and drive in comfortably, while retaining a full view of the road.
- Don't drive in reverse more than necessary.
- Don't drive a vehicle that emits excessive noise or fumes.

NB: There are other laws that a driver must know, for instance, about the loads a vehicle can carry, or when you can and cannot overtake. For a more detailed look at the laws of the roads, we recommend you read the relevant section in the Highway Code and ensure you understand *all* official signs and markings.

FINES AND ENDORSEMENTS

If you are stopped by the police, you may be given a 7-day ticket which asks you to present certain documents to a police station of your choice within 7 days. This will definitely be issued if you have committed an offence and are going to be charged. But, even if you haven't done anything wrong, don't argue. Failure to produce your documents can lead to prosecution. The police are simply checking that you are legally entitled to drive.

If you break a motoring law, there are two basic penalties. You can get a straight fine, or an endorsement on your licence and a fine. An endorsement is a penalty you have to carry on your licence for three years. Before 1982, three separate endorsements equalled a 6-month ban. Now, however, there is new system.

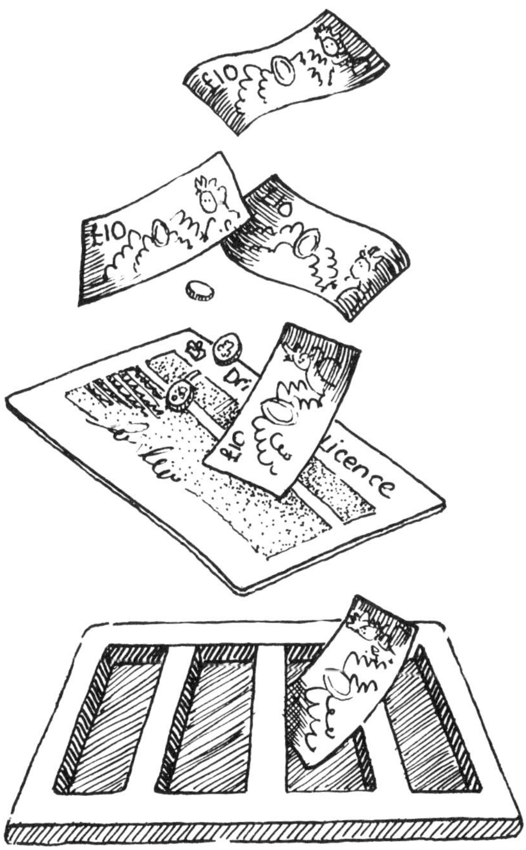

The 'points system' is a way of totting up offences committed over a three-year period according to the seriousness of their nature, rather than their number. For instance, breaking a speed limit is an endorsable offence which carries 3 points, whereas reckless driving, also an endorsable offence, carries 10 points. So you can see that the reckless driver's licence suffers more than the speed breaker's.

A total of 12 points on any one licence within a three-year period (starting from the date of the first offence and finishing with the date of the conviction for the last) qualifies for a 6-month ban. This does not have to be applied, however, and a 3-month ban or no ban at all can be decided by the court.

While most offences have a fixed point penalty, there are some that are left to the court's discretion, and others that receive an automatic disqualification – namely, drinking and driving, manslaughter, causing death by reckless driving, and racing on the highway. Any endorsable offence can warrant disqualification at the court's discretion, but circumstances don't usually make this likely.

For a complete list of the number of points given for various offences, you can apply to your local law courts, solicitor or police station. This will give you a clear idea of what common offences exist and what penalties they carry.

DRINK AND DRIVING

It's common knowledge that drinking and driving are a bad mix. So if you consume more than the limit allows, don't even get into your car. The law is so severe that even if you were found asleep in the back of your car (with the keys on you) with excessive alcohol in your blood, your licence would be in jeopardy.

The financial penalties for drinking and driving are perhaps the most severe of all. Fines of up to £2,000 can be imposed. You can not only lose your licence for a minimum of one year, but you can also lose the right to drive at all if it's a second offence. That means you're right back at square one, and have to take your test all over again! Imprisonment for up to 6 months is another possible part of the penalty.

How much you can drink before putting yourself over the limit depends on the individual, and is affected by your body weight, your rate of absorption and by how much you eat at the time of drinking. The actual limit is 80 milligrammes of alcohol in 100 millilitres of blood. As a guideline, the following could put you over the limit:

one and a half pints of beer
two glasses of wine
three single pub measures of a spirit

(Just one cocktail can sometimes put you over the limit on its own.)

If you drink more, and yet don't feel in the slightest bit intoxicated, don't fool yourself. The court will not be interested in how you felt at the time – only in how much alcohol you had in your blood.

If you are stopped by the police and asked to do a breath test, don't refuse. It will only mean that you'll have to go to the police station. And later, 'refusing to give a breath test' means an automatic loss of licence and could be added to any other charges.

The only safe maxim is *don't drink and drive.*

RECKLESS DRIVING

Reckless driving can carry almost as severe penalties as drinking and driving, and in bad cases it can carry worse. Reckless driving would include, for example, falling asleep at the wheel, ignoring a policeman's signal, racing another vehicle, driving excessively fast... In fact the list is endless because any driving that puts other drivers, pedestrians or property at risk is classed as reckless.

The penalties for reckless driving are a maximum £1,000 fine, and imprisonment for 6 months. Disqualification is left to the discretion of the court. If, however, a case goes on from the magistrate's to a crown court there is no limit to the fine that can be imposed, and there's the possibility of a 2-year prison sentence.

ACCIDENT PROCEDURES

If you are involved in an accident, be it serious or just a bump, there are a number of simple procedures to follow.

- Stop your car in a safe place where you are not causing an obstruction. Any other vehicle involved should do the same. If they don't, take any details you can, registration number, type and colour of car etc, and report the incident to the police immediately.
- *Never* apologise or make any judgement as to whose fault the accident was.
- Ask the other driver for his name, address, the name of his insurers, and his registration number. Supply him with the same information.
- Take note of the time, date, road conditions, signs and markings, and, if the accident was a bad one where there is likely to be argument over who was at fault, see if there are any witnesses who would be willing to testify.
- Take note of the damage to the other person's car and how severe it is.
- Having done all of the above, if your car is safe to drive, you may leave.

Remember to contact your insurance company as soon as possible afterwards. The next step will be theirs...

Sometimes there are other things to consider...

- If the accident involves another person or a horse, cow, ass, mule, sheep, pig, goat or dog (though, funnily enough, not a cat) rather than another vehicle, the same procedure applies. You must give your details to anyone who has reasonable grounds for needing them. If you do not have your insurance certificate with you at the time, inform the police of the accident and present it at a station within 7 days.
- If you crash into an unattended car or property, where it is impossible for you to exchange details with the owner, you are obliged to report the accident to the police immediately and in any case within 24 hours and to produce your insurance within 7 days.